Keeping
BEES

Keeping BEES

John Vivian

Illustrated by Liz Buell

WILLIAMSON PUBLISHING
CHARLOTTE, VERMONT 05445

Library of Congress Cataloging-in-Publication Data

Vivian, John.
    Keeping bees.

    Bibliography: p.
    Includes index.
    1. Bee culture. I. Title.
SF523.V58   1985   638'.1   85-26286
ISBN 0-913589-19-5

Cover and interior design: Trezzo-Braren Studio
Illustrated by: Liz Buell
Typography: Villanti & Sons Printers, Inc.
Printing: Capital City Press

Williamson Publishing Co.
P.O. Box 185
Charlotte, Vermont 05445
1-800-234-8791

Manufactured in the United States of America

14 15 16 17 18 19 20

Contents

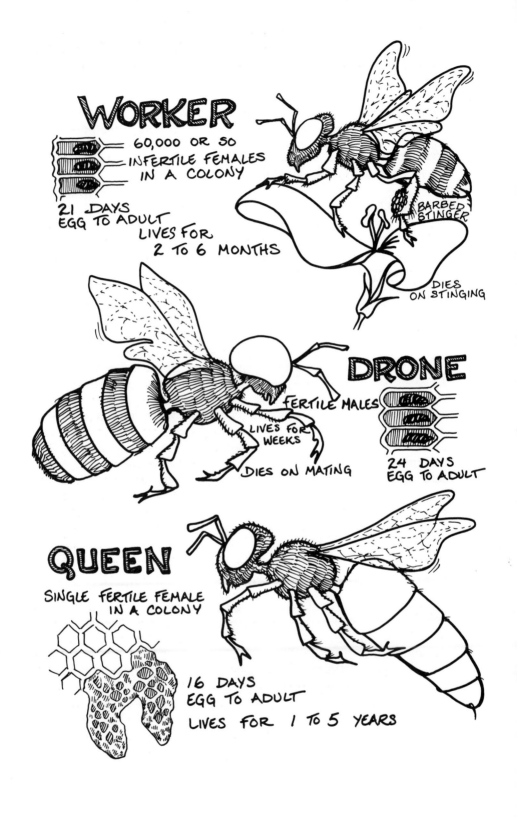

WORKER

60,000 OR SO
INFERTILE FEMALES
IN A COLONY

21 DAYS
EGG TO ADULT
LIVES FOR
2 TO 6 MONTHS

BARBED STINGER

DIES ON STINGING

DRONE

FERTILE MALES

LIVES FOR WEEKS

DIES ON MATING

24 DAYS
EGG TO ADULT

QUEEN

SINGLE FERTILE FEMALE
IN A COLONY

16 DAYS
EGG TO ADULT

LIVES FOR 1 TO 5 YEARS

Introduction

Keeping bees! The words conjure up a delicious picture, don't they? A fragrant spring day, an orderly row of gleaming white hives lined up along the garden fence, and bees, your own bees, buzzing happily in the flowers and turning out those perfect little squares of comb honey you find in gourmet food stores.

If the idea has you buzzing as it first did me some twenty-five years ago, you want to get to buying bee boxes and filling them with busy little nectar-collectors right away. But first, there's a great deal to learn about the fascinating life of these social insects and about the hives and equipment you will buy or build to manage them.

Beekeepers' woodenware is lovely stuff; it often smells of honey when you take the beautifully milled parts from the box. But it isn't cheap, and you can save cash by making some of it yourself. Plus, there are many strains of bee to choose from. So, even if you plan to obtain your basic equipment from the Sears catalog or a local beekeeping retailer, you should send away for a selection of free literature from the equipment suppliers listed in the back of this book.

The catalogs and price lists are an education in themselves. A postcard with your name and address on the back will do, and within the week you'll be browsing through page after page of Hoffman-frame Langstroth hives made in three sizes out of redwood, pine, or cypress in standard, economy, or commercial grades. Plus wired, plain, and plastic-based beeswax comb foundation, a whole arsenal of hive tools and smokers and beeveils, electric uncapping knives and solar wax melters and shiny stainless steel centrifugal extractors. Then there are the honeybees themselves: dusky gray Carniolans, bright yellow-banded Italians, gentle Caucasians, proprietary strains such as the Mraz or Buckfast, and hybrids like Starlines and Midnites. These are sent direct by mail in packages of 6,000 to 10,000 bees complete with a young queen and her attendants enclosed in a little private shipping cage plugged with bee candy.

While you're mailing away for the catalogs, you should also write for free samples of the beekeepers' magazines. Their addresses are also listed at the back of this book. You will want to subscribe to one or two to read news of the lively world of beekeeping: the always arguable opinions of longtime beekeepers mixed with latest academic research findings and discussions of topical issues such as the recent bee mite scare and the hotly debated impact of the African/Brazilian hybrid "killer bees." Events in the bee world's social schedule—conventions, shows, fairs, and meetings of local beekeepers' organizations — are described. Most include bee-beard contests that you'll be confident to enter with a little experience. First prize is likely to be a chaste buss on the cheek from the local Honey Queen plus a T-shirt reading "BE MY HONEY, BEE." Backyard beekeeping is unmechanized, low-tech, gratefully old-fashioned, and all good, clean fun.

The literature is guaranteed to get the garden season juices rising too, even in folks who have come to view seed catalog photos of perfect corn ears and dew-sprinkled tomatoes with the skepticism born of hard experience with borers and blossom-end rot. Indeed, keeping bees is often a fresh, new challenge for a slightly jaded home gardener, a first step beyond plant culture into livestock raising. And of course there's the prospect of sampling that first crunchy comb honey, flower-fragrant and golden as it pools with butter in the steaming center of a freshly baked muffin. Now that's a country-living-lover's thrill on a par with a first taste of your own green peas steamed with new mint, or slicing into a tomato so fresh off the vine it's still warm from the sun.

While the catalogs and magazines are in the mail, we'll point out a few potential neighbor problems you can avoid by picking your hive location carefully. Next comes selecting essential equipment and choosing the bee strain best suited to your needs.

Succeeding chapters will cover details of assembling equipment and installing your first colony of bees. Then we'll go step by step through the year, suggesting management practices to bring you the greatest satisfaction and optimum honey production. And, from time to time I'll introduce some of the fascinating lore that has been discovered in man's long association with the honeybee — information that won't concern you now but should prove helpful later in your beekeeping career.

Chapter 1

PLANNING
YOUR
APIARY

The first step in beekeeping is to find an out-of-the-way, yet convenient location for your collection of hives, your apiary—so called after the Latin name of the honeybee: *Apis mellifera*. Each colony will consist of 60,000 and more purposefully buzzing little *A. melliferae*, better than half of them making ten to a dozen foraging trips a day during the height of the honey season.

Bees on forage truly do make a beeline from food source to home, and they don't fly any higher than necessary. Pets, people, or livestock that move into a flight path can get bee hit.

Bees are not programmed to sting when foraging; they compete for nectar and pollen by hard work, by out-hustling the next bee on the flowers. Stingers are saved to defend the nest. Still, if your neighbor moves into a beeline when hoeing the broccoli, and a bee falls buzzing into her shirt, she may be stung. You must locate your hives so the bees won't interfere with other folks' activities.

Bees Need Water

In addition to the nectar bees make into honey and the pollen they feed the young, bees also collect water. If they decide to take it from the kids' wading pool, the pony's watering trough, or a leaky outdoor faucet, bees can become a real nuisance. They can be more than a nuisance to drivers on streets that border an apiary. If a bee buzzes into an open car window, she can cause panic or an accident, even though she wants only to escape and carry her load of nectar or pollen back to the hive. Vehicles can also take a considerable toll if your hives front a well-traveled road.

Pick a location where the hive entrance can be pointed away from human or animal activity. Suburban beekeepers usually put hives along the backyard fence, with entrances facing away from the garden or the kids' play yard. Try to aim the hives toward fields or orchards which will provide the major nectar supply and in the direction of nearby natural water sources. Lacking a stream or pond, locate the apiary near enough to the house that you can pipe in water or haul buckets easily.

Ideal Hive Location

Ideally, your hives should face open country and receive full sunlight in the mornings and throughout the day in cold weather. An obstruction-free flight path helps nectar-laden bees find their way home more easily. Like other insects, honeybees are cold-blooded, and become lethargic at temperatures much below 60° F. The sooner a night-chilled hive warms in the morning sun, the sooner the occupants will get to work.

During the flying season, bees clear their digestive systems at random in the fields. But in cold weather, they may be cooped up for weeks or months at a time, using rare warm and sunny days to make cleansing flights over short distances in front of the hive. The droppings are an unobjectionable dark yellow fluid, but dry into a kind of glue, and several thousand bees can severely spot the neighbor's drying bed sheets. Facing the hives into open country will avoid the problem, and a sun-warmed hive will encourage them out whenever possible in winter.

Facing the hive toward the south is conventionally recommended for the snow belt. However, beekeepers in northern Canada have found that a south-facing entrance can warm too rapidly and deceive the bees. They fly out into the still, sub-freezing air where they chill, become immobile, and die. Yukon beekeepers face hive sides or backs toward full sun.

A Bee Barrier

If you can't face your hives toward open country, place a high barrier ten or more feet out in front of the hives. You want a seven-foot or higher shrubbery screen or fence that will force bees to fly above person-height.

If screens are impractical, you might place hives in an attic, barn, or the top of a garage. Bees nest naturally in hollow trees, on cliffs, or in buildings well above the ground, so a second- or third-story location will suit them fine as long as fresh air can circulate around the hives in both hot weather and winter.

In the North, avoid placing hives in frost pockets where cold air will flow down, pool, and chill bees in winter, just as it frosts tomato or squash plants during the early autumn. Locate your hives part way down an east- or south-facing slope, if possible. Wind chill is a bee killer in snow country. When temperatures dip below 54° F., the colony begins to cluster to keep the queen and young at 93° F. In severe cold, especially with constant warmth-sapping wind, they cluster too tightly, won't move when honey stores are depleted, and die.

A windbreak is desirable in the North. A thick, old maple trunk will suffice, or you can put up a snow fence, pile hay bales to the wind side of the hives, or insulate the hives.

On our mountain, arctic winds come down direct and special delivery via Alberta, but the temperatures seldom fall below −10° F., and the wind chill to much under 50° below. Many local bee-keepers winter their colonies uninsulated and in the clear with no more than the expected 5 to 10 percent winterkill.

Danger of Heat

In the Sun Belt, you must protect your colonies from excess heat. At temperatures much above 95° F., bees slow down, and they stop flying at 110° F. To collect water to cool the hive, workers spread drops of water on the interior, then fan with their wings to evaporate the water and to blow the heat-absorbing water vapor from the hive. It's fascinating to watch them in hot weather—bees on one side of the entrance facing out and fanning air in, bees on the other side buzzing in reverse.

However, bee power alone may not be sufficient to cool a sun-baked hive on a humid August afternoon. The sun can beat the bees, wax can melt, and honey stream from the hive. If 90°-plus temperatures are common in midsummer where you live, be sure to provide summer shade. A friendly locust tree will do fine to filter out high, summer sun. Lacking trees, you can put the hives under a proper roof or a sun break of wood-lath or even an old-time ramada of vegetation laid over a pole framework.

A beehive in midsummer weighs 100 or more pounds, so choose a permanent location, or one readily accessible from the road if you intend to move hives often.

Bees naturally defend their approach area, which is a fan-shaped space reaching out perhaps fifteen feet in front of the hive, so you will be working from the hive back and sides. Leave full walking space around each hive, and place the hives at least six to eight feet apart.

Avoid Wet Site

Bees will drown in standing water, and will be unable to control inside temperatures if plagued by moisture in soggy soil beneath the hives. Also, hives are made of wood, which will rot. For these reasons, build a base to raise each hive above the highest possible water level. In flood-prone areas, you will want to put the colonies on permanent levees or platforms.

To avoid waterlogged soil and to bar termites, a solid base can be made from poured concrete, rocks, or cement blocks. In tropical areas, the voracious wet- and dry-wood termites are deterred with pottery hive bodies or by setting wooden hives on metal or ceramic pedestals, sometimes with moats of water or oil around them, or gummy "tanglefoot" applied between hive and ground.

We have no termites in the Berkshires, and the river hasn't reached the mountaintop yet, but a foot or two of mushy, wet snow can linger around a hive base for weeks into the spring, soaking it through. I place my hives on low, flat rock or cement block platforms, laid without concrete so they will drain well, and use cypress or pressure-treated wooden bases on top of the stone.

The stand and bottom board of a beehive are arranged on a base made of small cement blocks.

Hive bases should be level from side to side, so comb will hang straight, but have a slight downward slope – about a one-inch drop from back to front. As bees evaporate nectar into honey, a great deal of moisture is expelled. It may condense on the relatively cool baseboard of the hive and puddle there, soaking the wood. A slope will encourage it to drain off. The slope also keeps rain water from running into the hive.

Sources of Help

If you have any questions about the suitability of your climate or residential location to beekeeping, contact the local USDA/Cooperative Extension Service (the county agent) in your county seat. In Canada, look up the provincial apiarist. The government aggy people can fill you in on federal and state bee disease-control/hive inspection laws and will offer plenty of other help to boot, including the names of nearby beekeepers and the local beekeepers' organizations. Beekeeping groups are unmatched sources of good fellowship as well as practical hands-on information, and I heartily recommend that you join one. It's the best way to meet the experienced bee people who can offer details of weather, nectar flows, and other local beekeeping insights that no amount of reading can provide.

You'll find few areas of North America where bees can't be kept successfully. Beekeepers thrive in all fifty states including Alaska and in every Canadian province. Almost any climate, subarctic to tropical, will support bees, but a very few geographical areas won't. Unirrigated desert and high plains, deep forest or large urban complexes may support small populations of bumblebees or native solitary bees. But, their scant supply of flowering plants won't support a large colony of honeybees.

You *can* keep bees in the desert or in urban areas. It's even been done on a New York City roof garden. Indeed, flowering ornamentals in residential neighborhoods provide better honeybee forage than acres of golden and waving — but nectarless — grain. However, if the bees lack a steady nectar and pollen supply, you may put more into feeding your bees than they produce in honey for you. And there's nothing wrong with that if you're forewarned and willing to trade bought pollen substitute and Domino sugar for your own honey. At supermarket prices — about $1.50 per pound for honey, a quarter or so for sugar — you will at least break even.

If you are keeping bees in town, check your local ordinances; more than one municipality has anachronistic laws on the books declaring bees to be a public nuisance. An invaluable resource for urban beekeepers is the brochure *Beekeeping in Residential Neighborhoods*, free from the A.I. Root Company, Box 706, Medina, OH 44258-0706. It offers excellent suggestions for trouble-free hive location and for dealing with anti-bee ordinances.

Insecticides Are Dangerous

When evaluating your locale for suitability to bees, be alert to pest control programs. Many agricultural areas, and growing numbers of town yards and trees, are dusted or sprayed against insects. No farmer who relies on bee pollination will apply pest controls during blossom time. But not all farm crops, and no in-town ornamentals, are bee-dependent. Most chemical insecticides are lethal to bees, and if field workers aren't killed on the spot, they may carry the poison to the hive where it will destroy the developing young, or brood, as well as the young nurse bees that stay home tending the nest during their first three weeks after hatching. It may also kill the queen, who alone can lay fertile eggs to maintain the colony population.

You needn't worry about neighbors applying rose dust or spraying their apple tree. But, do know when large areas are being treated with commercial or agricultural insecticides, and be ready to protect your bees.

THE HIVE'S LOCATION

Here's a good hive location.

- It is sheltered from the prevailing wind (especially in the North).
- It is above standing water.
- It is faced so the flight of the bees will not be a nuisance to you or your neighbors.
- It is shielded from streets and activity areas by a barrier that will force the bees to fly up and over people, cars, and livestock.
- It is reached by the early morning sun. This gets the bees up and out to work, or to take cleansing flights as early as possible.
- Particularly in the South, it is shaded during the warmer parts of the day.
- It is on a southern exposure. It is not in a hollow, where the coldest winter air will settle.
- It is near a source of water, provided by the beekeeper if the nearest water source is your neighbor's swimming pool, a stock trough, or any other such source where bees would be a nuisance.

GETTING STUNG

If you keep bees, you can't avoid getting stung occasionally. If you are like 99.98 percent of the human race, you will experience nothing but a brief, sharp pain and a localized swelling that lasts only a few minutes, followed by itching for a day or two, particularly if the sting was on a joint or on thin skin over bone. Indeed, some people find bee stings an effective aid for symptoms of arthritis.

However, bee venom contains eight or more complex, little-understood, and variously toxic proteins, including minute amounts of a nerve poison similar to cobra venom. A very few humans are naturally allergic to the toxins, and a few more develop sensitivity with repeated stings. Somewhat under twenty people actually die in this country from honeybee sting reactions each year. Many more persons are stung by wasps and ground-nesting yellowjackets than by honeybees.

Most beekeepers become tolerant of stings, so in time they're almost immune to the poison. But it didn't work that way with me. After several years of beekeeping in the early 1970s, including the inevitable few stings, I foolishly handled a grumpy hive in bad bee weather (a cool, overcast afternoon with few flowers in bloom) and got a half-dozen stings on the head and neck for my trouble.

I suffered a mild case of anaphylaxis, the medical term for the body's reaction to a foreign protein encountered at least once before. My pulse became rapid, I could feel my face swelling, I felt faint, and found it more and more difficult to breathe. Scary. Unlike really severe cases of anaphylactic shock, my life was never in danger, but I was flat on my back for a few hours, endured forced retirement from beekeeping for several years, had to take a series of desensitizing shots, and still keep an MD-prescribed stinging insect kit in the refrigerator just in case.

I'd long been allergic to several foods and to airborne pollens, and might have predicted this bee sensitivity. Many people who are allergic to one thing may react to another. I don't pretend to know how allergies are interrelated, but my wife, Louise, and daughter, Martha, both have mild hay fever problems, and they find it easy to stay clear of the bees. Only son Sam seems to sneeze at nothing, and isn't fazed by a bee sting.

Don't let my experience scare you away. Only two people out of ten thousand need worry. Still, if you or anyone else who may tend your hives seems allergy-prone, a consultation with the family physician is in order.

NECTAR AND POLLEN SOURCES

Bees feed almost entirely on nectar and pollen obtained from blooming flowers, and flower nectar is where honey comes from. You should learn all you can about your local flower types and their blooming times so that you can order your first bees to arrive along with your earliest major pollen/nectar flows, and in later years, be able to time the colonies' spring buildup to match their food supply.

From the first flight in spring, each foraging bee concentrates on the most productive flower it can find in bloom at any given time. In search of the perfect flower, bees will fly up to five miles, but prefer to forage within a mile of home. The economic return from each trip—the time and energy consumed per unit of food brought in—diminishes if they must fly much farther.

Geology, topography, and vegetation in each square mile of bee country are different, and weather variations change the succession of bloom each year. For example, our last winter was mild and the spring was early but cold, wet, and dreary—rotten bee weather. Many flowers bloomed prematurely and were killed by spring frosts. Beekeepers call the incoming nectar a honeyflow, and this year our early flow was poor. Dandelions are the major source, and their blooming period was sporadic and brief. Weather remained cold during maple and tree fruit blossom, so bees couldn't fly, and apple nectar income was low.

Summer started off sunny, warm, and droughty. Berry blossom was extravagant, but clover, the major nectar source in good years, was waterstarved and mediocre. By early August, strong colonies had put up a good honey supply, but I didn't know whether any of it would be surplus to the bees' own winter requirements. Late summer provided heavy rains alternating with hot sun. The "blue flowers"—asters, chicory, and milkweed—ran riot, and the full-strength colonies packed the honey away. Fall was warmer and wetter than normal, too. The goldenrod bloomed profusely, and the bees worked overtime. What began as an unpromising year ended an unusually good one for our area.

The year before that, winter was about average, but otherwise temperature and precipitation conditions were reversed and so was the honeyflow. It came on in much lower quantities for an average spring and meager end of season.

In each of the two years before, we had brutal winters with a heavy snow pack and a long-delayed thaw. When the spring honeyflow arrived finally, it was a real rouser, and moderate rain and temperatures kept flows going through the year at adequate but not record levels. During one of those years there were no late spring frosts to nip buds. Our little orchard and seedling apple trees in the woods bloomed wonderfully for weeks of warm, good-flying weather, and the bees took full advantage. Wherever you live, no two seasons will be alike.

Nectar Sources

The flowering plants listed below are the most common nectar sources in continental North America. Hawaii's flora is unique, and beekeepers in the Islands are advised to visit the Cooperative Extension Service for information and a copy of *Fundamentals of Beekeeping in Hawaii (Ext. Bulletin 55)* from the University of Hawaii, Honolulu.

In a class by itself is:

White Clover. This is not the large red clover with sugary white tips at the bottom of pink florets that are too deep for honeybees, though bumblebees exploit them avidly. Look for white or yellow clover with small and inconspicuous heads in uncut lawns, farm pastures, and fields. It blooms all season and is the top nectar source when sun and rain are adequate. One or another species of Dutch white, alsike, or the little yellow sweet clover are found everywhere.

Other prime nectar sources, listed alphabetically, are:

Asters. Bees visit 200 and more species of this common meadow plant. Flowers are borne in clusters on tall spikes and have yellow centers and many thin petals in pale shades of blue and pink. Different species offer nectar year-round. This is primarily a mid-summer flower in our area. Its nectar produces a light, non-granulating honey.

Basswood. Horticulturalists call this the linden tree. It has heart-shaped leaves on long stalks, and fragrant, cream-colored flowers borne in sprays in late spring or early summer when other nectar sources may be drying up. Several species are native to the East, providing tremendous nectar flows in good years. Common cultivated trees, they are found continent-wide.

Berries. The many berry plants that flower spring to summer and fruit a few weeks later are good nectar sources. If you live in an area where bramble thickets are common, chances are they are berries.

Black Locust. This is a favorite lawn tree with lacy compound-leaved foliage and long, dry seedpods in the fall. Sweetpea-shaped white flowers grow in loose, hanging clusters about five inches long, and produce a sweet aroma and copious nectar in May and June most places.

Chicory. Alice-blue flowers borne close together along upright spikes are found growing on roadsides in late summer. Deep roots are roasted by country folks for a coffee substitute, and the plant offers a powerful nectar source for our bees continent-wide.

Cucurbits. Cultivated cucumbers, squash, melons, and their relatives have huge, yellow flowers that attract bees and offer a grand nectar and pollen supply the gardening season through. Commercial cucumber fields in the valley below us fuel hundreds of bee colonies.

Dandelion. Wherever this lawn nuisance rears its golden head, the pollen and bitter honey provide a major early spring growth-stimulant.

Fruit Tree Blossoms. Apples in our area, peaches in the South, wherever fruit trees bloom, the bees congregate, sometimes in such numbers that the whole tree seems to hum and shimmer in the early spring sun. Blossoms usually are too early to supply surplus honey.

Goldenrod. This is the major late-season occupant of many overgrown fields and roadsides, with its drooping yellow heads of many small yellow flowerlets. It's a fall sneeze-maker only if you put your nose right into the flower head. The pollen is sticky and falls when shed, so doesn't ride the winds and cause hayfever, contrary to popular belief. It does stick to bees, though, and the abundant, if bitter, nectar is a major fall nectar source everywhere but along the Pacific coast.

Maples. The familiar tall trees of many species flower inconspicuously each spring, growing everywhere but the Southwest. If weather cooperates, it provides tremendous amounts of nectar and pollen.

Mustards. These yellow-flowered, broad-leaved plants are found in every meadow and as a weed in grain fields. They are members of the brassica family, the same as cabbage and relatives, so are good eating if you can identify them and gather the leaves when they are small. The bees pick them out when the bloom is at its peak, and gather nectar and pollen throughout the summer.

Ragweed. This is the plant that makes the airborne pollen that causes much fall-season sneezing for people and provides much of the overwintering pollen supply (but no nectar) for our bees.

Vetch. This legume looks like a pea vine with its fuzzy, compound leaves and curly tendrils found underfoot in every field, as ground cover along roads and grown as livestock fodder. The pea-like flowers borne on little spikes are white or violet and the bees love 'em. Go barefoot in the meadow during vetch bloom and you may step on a bee hidden in the lacy foliage and receive an unexpected sting on an inconvenient place.

Willows. Early, pussywillow-like buds distinguish these trees that prefer moist soils. They are the earliest pollen source in our area and a great early nectar source most everywhere.

Warm Climate Plants

Citrus. This group easily supplies half of Florida's honey and much of it in California and Texas, though the fragrant, nectar-brimming blossoms do not need bees for pollination.

Cotton. This is a tremendous nectar source if you live near the fields and monitor insecticide applications. The honey granulates quickly.

Black Mangrove. This provides nectar along the Florida waterways, where it hasn't been crowded out by the high-risers.

Mesquite. This food source for all dry-country life provides a fabulous nectar source for bees when its five-inch flower spikes bloom from May to June.

Palmetto. It has encountered the same difficulties as the mangrove, but grows inland too.

Sourwood. This tree has smooth, slender seven-inch leaves and, in summer, ten-inch clusters of bell-shaped flowers that drive the bees wild. This makes a non-granulating honey.

Tupelo. The black or sour gum tree is one of the most luxuriant nectar-producers on earth from its single, greenish flowers. It's another southern tree that turns out honey that will keep without granulating if cured properly.

Study Your Flora

In your own locale, you may find the bees harvesting crops of mango or fireweed or catalpa or wild blueberry or manzanita nectar. Other areas proffer mixed wild flowers such as the sumac and milkweed that proliferate in our own back forty, or suburban ornamentals, or fields of buckwheat. Bees find nectar in poison oak, cranberries, mints, sage, and cactuses. And more.

During poor nectar flows, you may find frames filling with honeydew, the sugary secretions that aphids and other plant-sucking insects exude, in part to attract sugar ants, which transport them from plant to plant. Bees will take it, too, if flowers are scarce. Wholesome enough, it is a murky, off-flavored nectar that doesn't produce proper honey under USDA rules. It is fine for bees' current food supply, but isn't good for winter stores, though there's no way I know to keep them from harvesting or using it.

With substantial experience managing bees in your own locale, you will be able to predict nectar flows and time the growth of your colonies to match. By knowing nectar sources you can also predict storage qualities of honey, its tendency to crystallize or darken with age. Learning about the sources of bee food is almost as fascinating as studying the bees and their hive—the next step in beekeeping.

Chapter 2

BEEKEEPING
EQUIPMENT

From Mother Nature's stern point of view, a bee colony has but one job each year – to reproduce itself. This it does by swarming – flying off to a new home.

The package of bees you buy to start your own colony is an artificial swarm, bees shaken out of an active colony and united with a young queen, just-mated and eager-to-lay – a combination that makes a veritable nest-building machine.

Your hive must duplicate essential features of the bees' preferred wild homesite or they won't move in. Left to its own devices, the colony would seek a home that's well shielded from rain and wind and sturdy or high enough to be safe from predators. The most attractive locations are dark spaces with small openings – hollows high in trees, niches in cliffs, and upper story interwall spaces in buildings.

From the overhead of these natural sites, the bees suspend gently undulating, vertical curtains of wax comb. Each comb is made of twin sheets of horizontal, slightly upward-pointing hexagonal cells, laid out 4.83 to the linear inch and measuring 1⅜" from the midpoint of one comb to the midpoint of the next. There's a bee-width crawl space of ⁵⁄₁₆"—no more than ⅜", no less than ¼"—between each pair of facing combs.

The cells are used to raise the young and to store supplies, and the comb serves as home perch to tens of thousands of bees. Less than one two-thousandth of an inch thick, the comb depends on its geometry for its strength. A typical foot-long section of drawn comb will support over a thousand times its own weight.

THE HIVE'S HISTORY

Comb contains straight lines and geometric shapes—rarities in nature, and it has been a source of wonder to the inquiring mind of man since we left our fellow apes in the trees. Stone Age cave paintings and rock drawings depict bee hunters of 15,000 years ago gathering nature's most concentrated sweet. Present-day tribal hunter/gatherer peoples enjoy wild honey—comb wax, pollen, young bees and all. Reportedly, it has a nutty, granola-like flavor and provides about the same nutrients as a peanut butter and honey sandwich.

Domestication Failed

With the development of settled farming cultures, man tried to domesticate the honeybee as he had dogs and cattle. It didn't work; bees remain as wild as ever. But they have taught us to feed and house and manipulate them so they'll turn out honey where we want it—in hives rather than high up in trees—and, with luck, in greater quantity than they would produce in nature.

The first hives, developed in Europe and Africa where the honeybee evolved, were replicas of the bees' natural homes—hollow logs, or bark, or rush tubes plugged at the ends. Next came smaller and more easily transported hives made of wood slats, cork, or pottery, and the picturesque skeps of coiled, rush-sewed straw rope illustrated in honey promotions.

Apis mellifera was brought to the Americas in box hives and skeps by European colonists during the seventeenth century. Log hives, called "gums" in the South, were in use well into this century, though they are illegal now where bee disease legislation requires that colonies be easily inspected.

Killed to Harvest

The bee colony had to be seriously disrupted or killed with burning sulfur (brimstone, as it is called in the old bee texts) to harvest honey from the early hives. Beekeepers experimented for generations to develop a hive that could be opened and closed at will, with easily removable frames from which the egg-laying queen could be excluded so the bees would turn out combs of pure honey.

Langstroth Design

The design that has become a global standard was patented in 1851 by a Yale-educated Congregationalist minister, the Rev. Lorenzo Lorraine Langstroth. His book, *Langstroth on the Hive and the Honey-bee*, first published in 1853 and revised by him until 1875, was the first bible of beekeeping.

Langstroth discovered (or more correctly perhaps, popularized) the principle of bee space: inside their homes, bees insist on that $\frac{5}{16}"$ of workroom. In any area much larger than $\frac{3}{8}"$ they will build comb—honeycomb if there's space, and either useless burr or brace comb if there isn't. Any space much under $\frac{1}{4}"$ is filled with propolis, a tarry glue/sealant collected from tree saps and used to block holes and seal cracks in the hive.

Most features incorporated into today's hive were developed through trial and error by the Jeffersonian gentleman-scholar/farmers who were attracted to beekeeping in the nineteenth century. The modern hive combines the Langstroth hive body with ten Hoffman self-spacing frames. This design culminated decades of experimentation by upper-New York State beekeepers during the 1800s. It was perfected and popularized by entrepreneur A. I. Root of Medina, Ohio, and is sold today by the bee supply company that bears his name.

Each frame is a wooden rectangle that holds a sheet of beeswax comb foundation on which the bees construct their comb. The concept was developed in Germany and perfected in North America by Charles Dadant, founder of the Hamilton, Illinois, bee supply firm, Dadant & Sons, Inc.

Foundation

Foundation is a sheet of wax—some kinds containing imbedded reinforcing wires or plastic backing sheets—which is pressed between metal dies so it comes embossed on both sides with the cell pattern bees follow in constructing cells sized for raising workers. Bees will nibble the outer wax surfaces off each side of a frame of foundation, augment it with flakes of new wax the young bees produce under their lower abdominal lantes, and draw it into comb. A sheet of foundation will be completely drawn in only a day or two by a new swarm, the package of bees you will be introducing into your new hives, or by an established colony experiencing a good honeyflow.

Except in England, which maintains a proudly independent course in beeware, wooden hives, frames, and foundation around the globe are made to Langstroth-standard specifications. Bee space is maintained at the top of each hive body, compared to British designs which are bottom bee space hives. This is irrelevant to the bees but important to you when assembling hive components. Outer dimensions vary with wood thickness, but with U.S.-standard 1″ lumber planed to a silky smooth finish but only ¾″ thick, the standard hive body measures 16¾″ from side to side (width) and 19⅞″ from front to back (length).

The more critical inner area is 14¾″ wide and 18¼″ to 18½″ long, depending on the manufacturer.

Depths

There are several bee box depths. The box most commonly used for brood chambers is 9½″ deep (plus or minus up to a quarter-inch, depending on the maker). The same box is used for the standard super, a hive body used to collect surplus honey for extracting.

A standard super brim full of honey contains up to sixty-five pounds of very dead weight, and that's an armful. Many beekeepers use a smaller shallow super weighing a more manageable forty pounds or so when full. It is 5¹¹⁄₁₆″ deep, and is used both for extracting and for producing comb honey—the kind harvested wax and all in chunks cut from the frame. Section supers are used to turn out those beautiful round or square portions of comb honey the bees build inside wood or plastic frames and which sell at high prices in stores. These are 4¾″ high. The only other common size bee box is the Illinois Shallow or Dadant hive; at a 6⅝″ depth it's a cross between the standard hive and the shallow super.

Many Western beekeepers use standard-sized hive bodies for both brood chambers and honey production. In the East, most beekeepers prefer two standard bodies as the brood nest and put on shallow supers. Some folks like the Dadant mid-sized hives for both purposes, and others mix all sizes up in whatever combinations work best for their management system. I doubt that the bees care one whit.

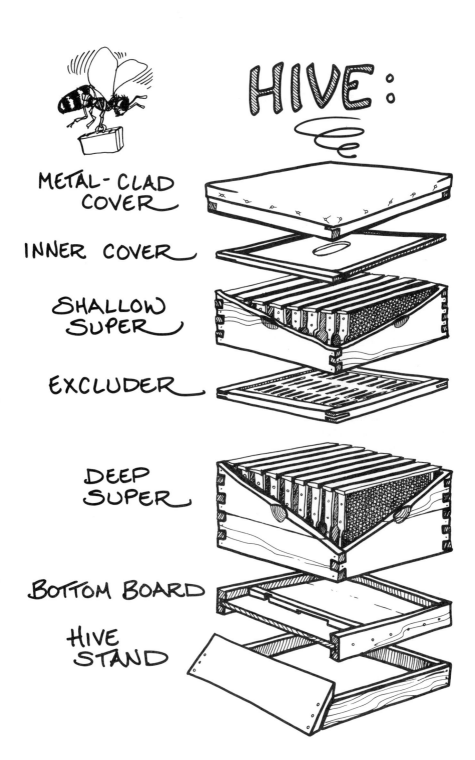

HIVE:

METAL-CLAD COVER

INNER COVER

SHALLOW SUPER

EXCLUDER

DEEP SUPER

BOTTOM BOARD

HIVE STAND

STARTER KITS

Most bee equipment suppliers sell a beginner's outfit—"everything you need except the bees." Typically, it contains a set of thick, sting-proof gloves with long sleeves attached. You'll discard those gloves as soon as their unwieldiness makes you drop your first bee-covered frame of honeycomb. There's a fancy bee veil to put on your (extra cost) bring-'em-back-alive, Frank Buck-style pith helmet, a book of instructions, a hive tool along with a standard hive with frames and foundation. Prices for these outfits range from a little over $50 to $100 or more, depending on quality and items offered in the kit.

When I started out some years ago, I opted for a high-priced beginner's outfit and learned the hard way that a second complete hive body ($25 and up) is needed in only a few weeks.

You'll also want at least two supers (another $40 or so) to produce surplus honey. Then there are the bees—about $30 for your first three-pound package—and the medications, books, and magazines you will surely accumulate over time. In other words, starting out with bees is going to set you back the better part of $200 per colony if you buy all your gear from a premium supplier.

Cutting every cost corner you can short of making your own hive bodies from home-cut lumber, you will still be out $100 per complete colony. Then, you will be adding equipment as your colonies grow (or diminish) and need to be divided (or combined).

Ads for some "beginner's outfits" are a little unfair if you are lulled into thinking it really is "all you need to start but the bees." Some companies sell complete outfits and make a point of not trying to disguise the total cost, but you are better off assembling your own outfit—taking the time to decide what you need and what you want to make yourself before you purchase anything.

HIVE EQUIPMENT

From the bottom up on the illustration leading off this chapter (and with prices given in '85–'86 U.S. dollars for kits, all beautifully precut and usually predrilled, but knocked-down—KD—so you have to assemble them yourself) the basic hive consists of:

Hive Stand

You must raise the hive off the ground to keep the insides dry. Cement blocks or wood beams will do, and no one really needs the illustrated hive stand—a rot-resistant cypress or red cedar frame with a sloping front landing board to keep overloaded workers from stalling out on the approach to the entrance slot and falling into the grass. This is strictly a hobbyist's item that no 1,000-colony commercial apiary can be bothered with. I use them if only for the design value. The gentle slope of the front board melds the vertical lines of the hive with the gentle contours of the earth, and I'd think it would make a more inviting entrance for any bee. Anthropomorphic nonsense, I admit. I've seen no scientific research to indicate that they do anything but relieve the hobby beekeeper of $5 to $7. Easy to make for a dollar's worth of pressure-treated lumber, but not as pretty.

Bottom Board (Reversible)

Not as simple-minded as it may look, and the result of many beekeeper-years of pragmatic, in-the-apiary research, the bottom board is a great deal more than a base to support the hive bodies.

It's made from variable-width slats of tongue-and-groove pine boards, wedged—preferably glued—into slots of the rails that form three sides. Rails protrude ⅜" above the two sides and rear on one face, ¾" on the other. The hive entrance is formed at the open end by the long, thin slit between the bottom board and the lower front edge of the bottom hive body.

With the lower rails up, there should be perfect bee space between the baseboard and hive bottom. Few beekeepers use the board this way. Most put the higher rails up to give plenty of in and out room to the thousands of eagerly foraging bees. The bottom board takes a beating from ground moisture. Cypress or red cedar lasts longest. It costs $5 and up.

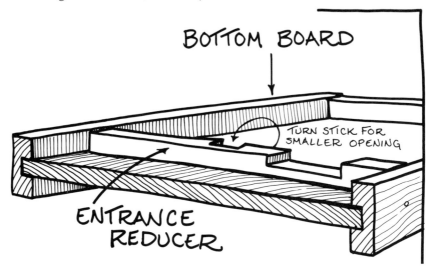

BOTTOM BOARD

TURN STICK FOR SMALLER OPENING

ENTRANCE REDUCER

Here are three sizes of hive bodies. Note the different construction of them. The top and bottom boxes have finger joints linking the sides, while the center one has a simple overlapping rabbet joint. The latter is easier to build, and thus is less expensive. Both are strong, if glue is used in the joints.

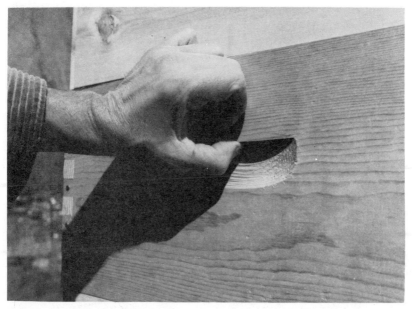

Here's my favorite hand hold, with a deep undercut that permits fingers to get a firm grip on the box.

Entrance Reducer

With the bottom board's higher rails up, the bees have ¾" of space for the entrance and under the comb. For bees just introduced to a hive, for all colonies from fall through spring, and any colony unable to defend itself any time of year, you must reduce the size of this entrance. Mice can invade the hive, and so can pest insects. But the main interloper will be bees from other colonies. When nectar is short, they'll gang up, overpower a weak body of guard bees, rob the hive dry of every drop of honey, and starve it out. Most bottom boards come with a wooden entrance reducer, a ¾" square, hive entrance-wide rail with two bee-high notches cut in. The smaller entrance, an inch or so wide, is for a new or very weak colony, the larger one at about 4" wide is for the new colony after a few weeks of brood raising. Plan to take the reducer out during the nectar season, then gradually reduce the entrance from late summer to winter. Cost is negligible. A handful of grass is an effective entrance reducer in an emergency, but will dry and fall out in time.

Hive Body

A 9½" deep top-and-bottomless box, or hive body, serves as the brood chamber, where the queen will lay eggs, the workers will raise the brood, and where they will put up stores to see the colony through the winter. Expect to pay $10–$25 per body with ten frames. Foundation will run about $10 more per hive body. Most beekeepers use two bodies per hive.

Super

Above the brood chambers (or below or between them—there are dozens of supering schemes you can try) come the supers for harvesting honey. During that delightful combination of a major nectar flow in a perfect honey year, a strong colony can fill ten or more 5¹¹⁄₁₆" shallow supers. Two per colony is the minimum you'll need. Cost is $18 and up with frames. Foundation costs $5 and up. Deep supers are also used for harvest.

Covers

All hives need a wind- and rain-proof cover. The prettiest one I've seen is the nicely sloping, gabled roof of the British W.B.C. hive, but you'd have to make your own if you want one to fit a Langstroth dimension hive. Commercial beekeepers in North America use simple and inexpensive—usually homemade—plank lids, but most backyard beekeepers use a two-part (inner and outer) cover.

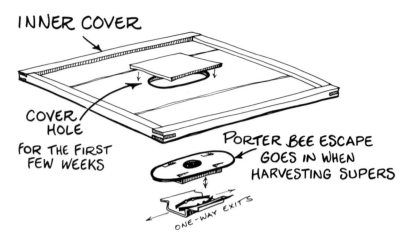

INNER COVER

COVER HOLE
FOR THE FIRST FEW WEEKS

PORTER BEE ESCAPE GOES IN WHEN HARVESTING SUPERS

ONE-WAY EXITS

Inner Cover

The inner cover goes on top of the bee boxes. It's made of thin lumber, plywood, or fiberboard set into wood rails. In better quality inner covers, one side is flat to provide exact beespace above the frames. Some have a small ventilating notch cut in the edge of the front rail to permit moisture to escape. All have an oblong cutout in the center to provide added ventilation. It will hold a Porter bee escape—a one-way portal inserted when the inner cover is placed under a super ready for harvest. Bees can leave the super but can't return.

Telescoping Outer Cover

The outer cover is a shallow box covered with sheet metal—galvanized steel or sheet aluminum. Old newspaper plates can be used on homemade tops. It telescopes down over the inner cover and top few inches of the top hive body to keep out wind and rain. You can open and inspect the hive any time of year, and the telescoping cover will snug down over the inner cover and hive body to seal the hive against the foulest weather—protection not possible with simple plank covers. The two-part cover is costly at $12 to $17, but worth the expense to backyard beekeepers who inspect their colonies frequently in all seasons.

Inside the Hive

All you really need inside the hive between bottom board and cover is the framework for your bees' construction, the frames and beeswax comb foundation. You can make or buy modern versions of accessories which were dreamed up by experimenters in the 1800s such as hive-sized feeders and slatted bottom racks which I like, queen/drone traps which I don't use but which some folks find help to control swarming, and the most controversial gadget in bee-dom, the pollen collector.

Frames are thin wood rectangles that hold the honeycomb. Most sold today are the Hoffman self-spacing pattern that automatically maintains proper space between frames. All are made with one or another version of the Root-design self-locking top that strengthens the frame. Brood frames and hobby-grade super **frames** have a ¾" thick top bar with a long wedge almost-but-not-quite cut out along one bottom edge. The bottom bar of the frame is grooved or split to hold the lower edge of the foundation. You cut out the wedge, lay the top edge of the foundation in the notch where the wedge was, then slip its bottom into the bottom bar and nail the wedge back with brads.

Some commercial honey producers use a thin top bar for their extracting supers. This gives a bit more comb space per frame, but requires welding foundation in place with melted beeswax — something you may want to do in time, but not right away.

Foundation comes in several styles. Simplest is the pure, thin wax foundation used for cut comb honey production. You eat it along with the honey, so it is installed as is, without any reinforcement.

Brood comb must stand up to years of bee traffic and human manipulation, and must be reinforced to withstand high temperatures that may cause it to slump or even melt. Combs for extracted honey must withstand the repeated stress of the extractor. So you want to reinforce all foundation that isn't to be eaten. Hundreds of comb-strengthening schemes have been dreamed up, and old bee literature is full of them.

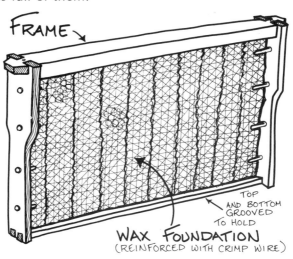

FRAME

WAX FOUNDATION
(REINFORCED WITH CRIMP WIRE)

TOP AND BOTTOM GROOVED TO HOLD

Today, unless you reinforce your own or order from overseas, your choice is from the following:

1. Plain Wax Foundation. This is liked best by the bees, no matter what anyone says, but it isn't strong enough for use in the brood chamber or when you are extracting surplus honey. Buy it for cut comb honey.

2. Wired Foundation. This is made in many styles. The most popular today is a Dadant origination having ten vertical wires embedded in the wax, each bent in a zigzag, crimped pattern, with small outward-projecting hooks at the top. You push the hooks up against the top bar with the wedge as you nail it on.

You'll noticed that each sidebar of the frame contains two to four holes. To hold the foundation in place, you can push little brass grommets or eyelets into the holes, then string horizontal wires across the foundation. The wires are then pressed into the wax with a heated wheel. This is most commonly used for commercial extracting operations or by the serious hobbyist.

Most hobbyists use support pins, made like small metal versions of old-time, split-dowel clothespins. You poke them through the holes in the sidebars after the foundation is in place. The foundation fits between the split ends. Wired foundation is stronger than plain wax, but the bees know it contains alien material, and will try to gnaw the metal out of undrawn foundation during slow nectar flows.

3. Three-layer Foundation. This has three separate layers of pure wax compressed under pressure into a plywood-like comb base. It is a specialty of the A. I. Root Company which recommends it even for extracting, where the danger of breakage is highest. It is not as strong as wired foundation, but it will resist malformation better than the plain.

4. Three-ply Plastic Center Foundation. In the Dadant version, trade name "Duragilt," wax is bonded to a plastic sheet, and the sheet is edged with metal. It has no support wires to bother the bees, but they know there's something wrong here, too, and will opt for the pure article every time.

5. Artificial Comb. The whole double-sided comb is molded in plastic by a number of enterprising entrepreneurs, and even the major manufacturers have started selling it. It is sold as is or with a thin beeswax coating. It is expensive, but will last forever. If you can get your bees to accept it, please tell me how.

OTHER EQUIPMENT

You'll need a few other pieces of equipment, and doubtless over time will accumulate a lot more you may not use every day, but which make the hobby more enjoyable. Here's the basic kit.

Hive Tool

This small scraper-end prybar can be purchased in most hardware stores. The bee supply houses sell chrome-plated ones as gift items, and there are several proprietary designs that you may want to try. A conventional crowbar is too thick for the delicate work of frame manipulation and hive scraping, and don't plan to use an old screwdriver or your pen knife. The hive tool is made for the work. $2 to $7.

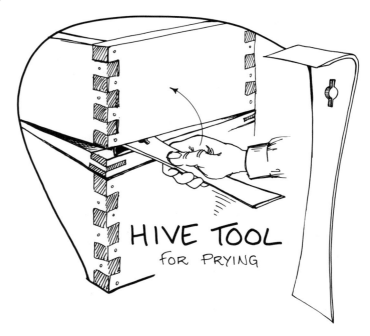

HIVE TOOL
for PRYING

Veil

A head net keeps bees out of your hair and off your face, with a long tail to tuck into your collar to keep them out of your shirt, too. Worn over a wide-brimmed hat, the net will make you look like a regular beekeeper, and the hat brim will hold the veil and any hostile bees on it well away from your nose. There are nets with plastic windows, little sewed-in holes for a pipe to project, and all kinds of other refinements. The complete outfit can set you back $20.

Smoker

The effect of smoke on bees has been known for thousands of years. The bees duck into the hive and gorge on honey which distends their nectar-storage sacks, making it hard for them to bend and sting. The smoke tends to pacify them, too. Smoke also masks chemical alarm signals like the banana-oil odor released by a stinging bee which calls in the others, stingers at the ready.

An aerosol bomb good for a dozen or two hive openings costs about $5 and is a good backup for a conventional live-fire smoker.

A bellows-driven smoker will cost $15 to $20. Get the big size (10" high), not the 7" model, which contains too little fuel to stay lit long enough for the slow-moving beginner. Don't buy extra "disposable fire chambers" that hold the fire inside the smoker. They are nothing but tin cans with one end cut out, the other punched full of holes. Recycle your V-8 juice cans.

Feeders

Beginner's outfits often come with a Boardman feeder, a little font that lets bees sip sugar syrup from tiny holes in the lid of an inverted Mason jar at the hive entrance. You invert the jar into a well on the feeder top, and the bees crawl under and sip syrup as they need it. A tight lid maintains a vacuum so the syrup won't pour out. With the entrance feeder you needn't break into the hive, which you shouldn't do for several days after introducing a new queen.

The Boardman is fine for package bees until nectar flow begins the first spring. Made from wood, plastic, or metal, it's sold for $2–$3. But, as it's outside the hive, the syrup is susceptible to thickening or freezing in cold, or fermenting in warm weather. Also, later in the year, the easily accessible food will attract robber bees.

A good added investment is a division board feeder for each hive. This is a thin plastic or wood and fiberboard tank that holds three pints and is put in to replace a frame for a time. About $4–$5. A larger model replaces two frames and holds five quarts. Other designs include gallon pails with little holes in the lids that you can invert inside a hive body and place at the top of the hive, plastic bags to put around a frame, and the most effective but costly, pressure sprayers that fill drawn but empty comb with honey.

My favorite is Dr. C.C. Miller's feeder, described in his wonderful 1915 book, *Fifty Years Among the Bees*. It's a super, divided down the center and holding over 1½ gallons per side. Bees can crawl up the center chute to feed at any time of year the temperature permits. Once a catalog staple, but missing for years, it's now back on the market in a modern version that's assembled, painted, and sold by the Quebec firm ARTB, Inc.

Queen Excluder

A $5 welded wire, plastic, or stamped sheet metal grid providing a .16" space through which workers can pass, but which will exclude drones and a laying queen with her enlarged, egg-filled abdomen. Don't try to make this in a home workshop. The tolerances must be precise and remain so.

Put the queen excluder between the brood chamber and the supers to keep the queen from laying eggs in the supers. Some beekeepers call these excluders "honey excluders" because workers resist walking on the plastic or metal, or squeezing through the openings. This problem is reduced by using the more expensive Root design that binds a wire grid in wood slats. To date, no all-wood model has been able to retain the crucial space tolerance in the moist hive atmosphere.

You'll need one excluder per colony, or two if you work the more complex supering systems.

Bee Brush

This soft-bristled little brush is used to swish bees off filled frames for harvest. It costs only $2.50 or so, and is a quick, cheap, and easy tool to use to get your share of the honey. The bees don't mind being brushed off one bit; they roll off the frame like bubbling, buzzing taffy and drip down into the hive.

INESSENTIALS—BUT NICE

Beekeeper's Coveralls

Made from white, sun-reflective material like lab workers' outfits, but with elastics at leg and sleeve bottoms to keep bees from crawling inside for an inevitable sting. Many have veils that can be zipped on or off. Coveralls can be a blessing for a large-scale beekeeper working during August in out-apiaries, hive collections put out at distant locations. They have lots of pockets to hold tools and record books, so they make a traveling office you can hang up in the shed at day's end. A $50 luxury for the hobbyist, but they will make you look and feel like a beekeeper.

Frame Grip

A spring-loaded clamp that costs $6 to $9 and gives you a one-handed grip to lift frames from the hive. I am short the ends on a couple of fingers of my right hand, and find the palm-squeezable grip to be invaluable in rapid manipulation of frames during a queen search or inspection for disease.

Extracting Equipment

This equipment is expensive. First, you'll need an uncapping knife to cut the cappings from the surface of the combs.

A two-frame, plastic bucket, hand-cranked extractor built like an old ice cream maker costs $180, and prices go up to thousands of dollars for a commercial honeyroom. A real extractor, a ten-frame, powered machine that will do the job quickly, costs over $700.

The Dadant catalog lists its own extracting gear. Most other suppliers sell equipment made by Maxant Industries, PO Box 454, Ayer, MA 01432. Send for Maxant's catalog even if you don't want an extractor. It has a dandy selection of metal accessories including stainless steel smokers.

A reprint of a clever extractor design using an old outboard motor bottom drive for the gear works, first published in *Gleanings in Bee Culture*, can be found in issue 68, March/April, 1981 of the *Mother Earth News*. From BACK ISSUES, TMEN, PO Box 70, Hendersonville, NC 28791.

The Pollen Trap

This $25+ device collects pollen by forcing the bees to enter the hive through a hardware cloth grill that scrapes the pollen from their legs. The pollen then drops into a tray beneath the grill.

You don't need this device unless you want to collect several pounds of pollen to feed your bees in the early spring. You will see ads by the trap manufacturers offering to buy pollen. They are traps set for your money. Let me digress a bit to explain why.

Promoters of bee products as human food surface with depressing regularity to gull beekeepers and consumers alike. Now that North America's perennial infatuation with fad diets is complemented by a physical fitness craze, a few exercise-prone celebrities are boosting their book and videotape sales by endorsing bee pollen as a way to lose weight, get sexy, or otherwise feel good without working at it.

There **is** an old popular belief based on a considerable body of anecdotal evidence (but as yet no scientific proof) that the small amounts of pollen contained in honey can help some folks with the spring- or fall-season sneezes. I like to think it helps me through maple pollen time, though why eating months-old, honey-cured, and inactive pollen would keep one from sneezing when the fresh and fully allergenic article is breathed in, I can't imagine.

My MD friends will accept only a possible "placebo effect"— where sick people often feel better after taking a sugar pill when

This pollen trap is mounted under a hive body. My thumb is hooked over the tray, pulled part way out. Bees fly through a crack left when the tray is closed, then move up through the screen mesh, which knocks the pollen off them. The little stick that's angled out lets bees bypass the trap. Shoddily made with cheap wood and soft metal staples, this trap isn't worth its cost of more than $25.

they believe that it is effective medication. Pure mind-over-matter and not to be sneezed at if it works.

But sugar pills are sugar pills, and honey is the same as sugar from a human nutrition point of view—tasty, but pure energy or empty calories, depending on how you want to phrase it. Other bee products lack any proven value at all in human health or nutrition and some pose potential hazards.

Royal Jelly Bust

There was a royal jelly boom in the 1950s that ruined many ingenious beekeepers who believed the promoters and invested heavily in queen-raising equipment before the bubble burst. Royal jelly is queen bee food. It takes 120 queen cells to produce an ounce of royal jelly; figure the labor cost of raising and harvesting that.

Royal jelly promotions haven't disappeared. But these days, it's pollen that promises the fastest money. A strong colony in a good year harvests about fifteen pounds of pollen – and can be encouraged to bring in more if much of its production is taken by the beekeeper, who could easily be tempted by an offer of "$$$ a Pound for Pollen, When Honey Brings ¢¢ Cents." And, sad to say, even in the space age some consumers can be led to believe that beebread is better for humans than an honest meal of fried chicken, potatoes and gravy, with fresh peas and a big salad.

It isn't.

As the USDA put it in its magazine, FDA Consumer, April, 1984, "Bee pollen is excellent food – for bees." A mixture of pollens contains an adequate balance of protein, vitamins, and minerals, but only part of the carbohydrate requirement (honey supplies the rest) for the developing young.

If you are tempted by either the buying or selling end of the pollen trap, consider the following observations summarized and freely paraphrased from the USDA article:

1. Pollen has no place in human metabolism except to cause some people to sneeze, itch, or have asthma attacks.

2. Since pollen hasn't been proven positively harmful to the non-allergic, it can be sold as food or a food supplement, so long as it satisfies pure food and drug regulations and does no actual harm.

3. Promoting any therapeutic benefit makes pollen a drug and subject to FDA testing and licensing, which it isn't and hasn't been.

In addition, despite frequent claims to the contrary, pollen is NOT:

*A bacteria-free germ killer; indeed, it loses its potency in a matter of hours and rots rapidly. Even the promoters tell you to freeze it immediately to prevent deterioriation.

*"Nature's Most Perfect Food," or "The Richest Source of Protein Known to Science." It's from 9 to 40 percent protein depending on flower source, at best having about the same food value as lentils, beans, or any other vegetable protein.

*An age retardant for people in the Caucasus region of the Soviet Union. Some folks there do live long lives hiking the mountain trails but pollen isn't so much as mentioned in a thorough study of their diet.

*A scientifically proven cure for hay fever, asthma, and other allergies. Indeed, as noted above, it causes allergic reaction in some people.

*An aid to athletic performance. Studies at Louisiana State University showed it had no effect at all.

*Anything special because it is the male seed of plants; so are corn tassels, bullrushes, and goldenrod tops, and no one promotes them as health food.

Besides, we're already taking the bee's honey. Why add insult to injury and rob the pollen they need to raise young bees? For heaven's sake, we often need to supply pollen or·pollen substitute along with syrup in the spring to build up colonies for the main honeyflow. Dr. A. Deitz, University of Georgia, suggested that pollen-trapping can reduce a colony's population by one-third. And as retired Tucson Bee Lab specialist Steven Taber III puts it (in "Pollen and Pollen Trapping," *American Bee Journal*, July, 1984) "If you put on pollen traps, you should expect certain hive problems that you don't have without them. Don't hurt your bees . . ."

YOUR FIRST SHOPPING LIST

Here is a realistic list of equipment you will need to get your bees off to a strong start and manage them until it is time to put on honey-harvesting supers. A list of supering supplies will come later, after supering options are discussed.

For each colony you plan to start—and I recommend that you begin with a minimum of two:

- 1 hive stand
- 2 full-depth hive bodies
- 20 top-quality lock-top, self-spacing brood chamber (full-depth) frames
- 20 sheets of wire-reinforced or multiple-layer brood comb foundation to fit your frames
- 80 metal support pins
- 1 bottom board
- 1 inner cover
- 1 metal-clad telescoping outer cover
- 1 Boardman entrance feeder and Mason jar to fit
- 1 plastic division board in-hive feeder
- Paint or stain for the hives (white latex exterior-grade paint is traditional, though I use a brown stain)
- 1 three-pound package of bees with queen. (Your choices in bee strains will be discussed in the next chapter.)

- 10 pounds white, granulated sugar
- Important accessories include:
  —a hive tool
  —a bee veil
  —gauntlet bee gloves if you don't have a pair of long leather gloves
  —a large-capacity bee smoker (stainless steel is best)
  —a soft bee brush
- Optional equipment, but nice to have:
  —an extra box of ten sheets of reinforced foundation
  —a frame grip
  —brad driver, helps getting those tiny nails into frame wedges
  —white coveralls to be your beeyard office

Chapter 3

BUILDING
AND
STOCKING
THE APIARY

By now your mail order literature has arrived, you've talked with a local beekeeper or two, picked up a Sears catalog, and perhaps located the nearest Dadant or Root outlet. It's time to order and assemble hives, pick a strain of bees, and schedule their shipment.

Plan backwards from arrival of the bees. If you are obtaining bees locally, take the supplier's advice on the best time to install them. Most mail order bee suppliers are in the South, where it becomes too hot to ship bees by late spring. It is too cold to ship much before early spring, so there is a tremendous rush from March through early June. To assure delivery during the rush, try to place orders before the first of the year. Ask the supplier to ship the bees to arrive as soon as your first pollen and nectar appear and about sixty days before the main honeyflow. That's how long a new colony needs to get up to operating strength.

For our part of New England and the rest of the snow belt, clover blooms toward the middle of June, so bees should come when maples are blossoming, pussywillows are making pollen, and I'm sneezing my head off—at the end of April plus or minus two weeks depending on the year, your altitude, and other geographical imponderables that only an experienced local beekeeper can resolve for you. In the midlands—North Carolina Piedmont and environs west through northern California, bees should arrive in early April (plus or minus two weeks). In the Deep South, you can order as early as you like. The upper reaches of Canada and the Alaskan Panhandle are two weeks behind New England, but many Canadian beekeepers install bees in mid-April, spring snowstorms or no.

All package bees need feeding until hive strength builds and flowers bloom. Consult a local beekeeper for best advice on timing to match the honeyflows. The best published information on regional honeyflows that I've come across is the USDA's National Honey Market News, address in the source list. A year's worth of back issues will help an isolated beginner to plan an entire year in the beeyard from package bee installation to buttoning up for winter.

Nucleus

A local beeperson may offer you a started colony made up of frames split out from active hives as a swarm control measure. This mini-hive is called a nucleus or nuc and should sell for $25 to $35 — about the same as you'd pay for a three-pound mail order package of bees. The nuc box is a small cardboard or wooden hive containing two to five standard frames with stores and brood, bees to cover, and a laying queen. If the queen came from a proven breeder, a nuc can get you started in a hurry—perhaps in too much of a hurry, so you'll have a full and swarm-prone colony before the main honeyflow. However, don't risk your beekeeping future on someone else's nuc with an amateur-bred queen even if it is cheaper; that's bad economics. Be sure, too, that your supplier's apiary is free of disease. Nucs can't be shipped through the mails, so sales are limited to the carry-out trade. Few nuc suppliers are large enough to be state-certified, so you are taking chances with disease and parasites.

Advance Notice

Mail order breeders will send you an order confirmation, promising delivery within a given week, though shipments are frequently delayed by the weather. Have your apiary assembled and ready to go—paint dry, frames assembled with foundation mounted, and hive bases set before the occupants arrive. Don't leave empty hives

Sam peers into a queen-breeding nucleus hive made by ARTB of Canada. It comes complete with half-size frames and an inside feeder. I use it to brood up queens from swarm cells removed from colonies in the spring and for holding new queens until they are needed for requeening.

A Boardman feeder can be used to feed a small colony in a five-frame nucleus hive. I made the entrance block from a piece of 1"×4" lumber to hold the feeder in place.

open and outdoors, especially with foundation in them. You will beg invaders of all sorts, and on a sunny day in an unoccupied, thus unventilated hive, the wax can get warm enough to slump, even in the spring.

You can buy equipment assembled and painted traditional white from most retailers and some mail order sellers. The cost is a little less and shipping is a whole lot less if you buy gear knocked-down (KD), and spend some time with a hammer, nails (supplied with nearly all equipment), and a good glue (never supplied, but strongly recommended).

ASSEMBLING THE EQUIPMENT

For assembly, you'll need a workbench, a small and a large hammer, a brad driver, assorted nails, a carpenter's square, and a large container of water-resistant carpenter's glue. Waterproof resin glue that will hold in the high-humidity hive environment is sold by some woodenware makers. A resorcinol boat-builder's glue is best, but Elmer's carpenter's glue will do, in my experience.

Sources for equipment are your choice and I hesitate to list my own preferences, except to suggest that you can save money by shopping around and trying the lesser-known manufacturers, though many require that you supply that strange commodity in today's charge-card economy—cash. Some favorite equipment is identified in the photos and construction tips, but there is no single best source for everything unless you let Sears or another major buyer do the choosing for you.

Bee woodenware is made to universal size and dimension standards, and isn't all that difficult to mill out, so is pretty much the same from brand to brand. Some makers sell on the basis of their name, others on service or convenience, and others on price. If you look hard in the catalogs, you'll find that each maker offers one or two unique features such as hive bodies of cypress (a wood that's rot-resistant though hard to get nails through without predrilling), proprietary frame designs such as the Western half-size, new ideas in woodenware joinery, even cute printed T-shirts and honey labels. All the non-standard gear is described with good points duly accented in the literature and bad points that you are left to discover yourself.

Quality in all brands can vary over time as sellers switch makers and makers update machinery or modify manufacturing quality standards or switch wood suppliers. Lumber quality varies even within the same formal grades. You usually have a choice among clear lumber (premium grade), wood with small sound knots (commercial grade), and economy grade that's sold in large lots and often needs reworking. I find that price differences among grades of a given maker aren't as significant as differences among makers. As in most commerce, a top name usually means quality, though not necessarily the best value for the dollar.

Even in the name brand premium grades, wood is sometimes a little warped and finger-joints of supers and lock tops of frames are hard to get together. This is seldom a function of brand; most mills use similar, quite simple equipment. (Indeed, anyone with a table saw can cut out hive bodies, though few beekeepers do, as the cost of raw materials bought at your local retail lumber yard can exceed cost of finished hive bodies.)

Top-quality boxes fit perfectly when freshly milled, but even clear, kiln-dried Maine or Oregon pine can swell or shrink over time. Moisture content of the wood when milled plus amount of time and humidity and heat in storage make the difference between easy and moderately difficult assembly. At worst, you'll have a few tight joints and perhaps split the thin top rail when nailing up a super—nothing that will affect the box's utility.

Before tackling the woodenware, though, you should order your bees so you'll have a due date to get the hives finished and in place.

PICKING YOUR BEES

Don't be tempted as I was years ago to save $25 and order only a queen, thinking that she'll behave like a wasp or bumblebee and start a nest single-handed. Honeybees gave up the solitary life when they became social insects some eighty million years ago. Queens **are** sold singly, and sold by the thousands for from $6 to $10 each, but strictly as replacements or to start colonies from bees and brood split out from an established hive. Once bred, a queen's prime function is to lay eggs, which she does at the rate of 1,000 to 2,000 per day. But she can't care for her own young or clean the house or bring in the groceries.

The workers produce all the income and do the housework, so you must get a package of several thousand workers to tend the chores. A two-pound package is sufficient for most North American locales, though a three-pound package may be desirable in the North if your thaw-to-nectar flow season is particularly short and you must build colony strength in short order. This is the case with much Canadian beekeeping where colonies aren't overwintered, but all honey is taken and colonies are rebuilt from new package bees each spring. Breeders who ship large quantities of bees to Canada select for quick strength-building. Their strains may grow so fast they would swarm in warmer latitudes.

You upper-U.S. and Canadian beekeepers are well advised to order bees trucked up by a local bee equipment seller, even if they are raised in Texas. Ask locally for the name of a reliable breeder whose bees are selected specifically for the Great White North.

Many breeders require all or part payment in advance to reserve bees during the busy season. Others will trust your phone order—one time. Charging on a credit card will save the time for a check to clear, if the breeder takes plastic money.

THE COLONY

There are three castes of bees in an active colony:

1. The queen, who emerges after only sixteen days from a normal fertilized egg. She is raised in a special queen cell on a special diet, for one of two life roles, as a supersedure queen raised to replace a dead or failing queen, or as a swarm cell queen raised to populate new colonies or to remain in the hive when the old queen leaves with the swarm.

2. Workers, infertile females which emerge in twenty-one days from fertilized eggs laid in conventional cells and which number in the thousands.

3. Drones, fertile males raised from unfertilized eggs in twenty-four days, in large, dome-capped cells and numbering several hundred in mating season, none in the winter cluster.

The Queen

The queen is the only fertile female in the colony, and is an egg-laying machine that sustains colony population in the tens of thousands by laying up to 2,000 eggs a day in peak season.

Additionally, through at least two pheromones and two added scents, one from glands at each end of the body, she governs her colony in what Edward O. Wilson, in his marvelous book, *The Insect Societies*, calls a "gentle despotism."

The key to the quality of your colony is the genetic material carried by the queen. She is mother of every bee in the colony once the package bees die out in a month or so, and every worker bee will carry her genes and those of the drones she mated with on nuptial flights from the apiary. Fully controlled in-flight mating can take place only in a research facility's flight room, and hasn't been all that successful anyway. Artificial insemination is easily done by a skilled beeperson, but such queens are not sold commercially.

Natural mating takes place in the air over an assembly point where all the drones and queens from a given area gather year after year. During mating flights of about a half-hour on six to a dozen succeeding days, a young queen gathers some six to twelve million sperm from several drones. It's her lifetime supply. The sperm are stored in layers in an organ called the spermatheca and portioned out as they come up, meaning that a queen's offspring will have a succession of fathers over her productive life. She may be from the sweetest, most congenial strain there is. But success in mating goes to the fastest flying and most aggressive drones. You may find your bees changing color, temperament, and working habits over the year. If they are consistently unruly or lazy or prone to disease, you may want to replace the queen. The undesirable traits may vanish as one particularly unpleasant drone's sperm is used up and supplanted by another's. This variability can also affect the basic strains of all but the most meticulous breeders, those who assure a good supply of desirable drones for their flying queens, who maintain apiaries in island-like isolation, and who control nearby wild colonies.

Characteristics of a breeder's entire strain can change in a single year, and the only guarantee that a brand of bees will be consistently good is the apiary's reputation and the stake it has in maintaining that reputation.

Again, the best source for information on breeders whose stock does well in your area is a successful local beekeeper. Failing that, you can rely on the breeders picked by the equipment makers, large truckers of bees to the north country, and by Sears. I've used Sears bees to start apiaries in several locales over the years and have never been disappointed. The most recent lot, ordered for a central New England location, came via Sears from the York Apiary, Jesup, GA 31545.

STRAINS OF BEES

The Western honeybees sold in the Americas and Europe are races of the single species *Apis mellifera*, and most probably evolved from the more primitive Asian or Eastern honeybee, *Apis cerana*, with which it can no longer interbreed successfully. All strains of *A. mellifera* are capable of interbreeding.

Italians

A. m. ligustica Spin. is the most popular strain in North America. These bees evolved on the warm Italian peninsula where winters are mild and the nectar season is protracted, so they maintain large populations through the year and into the winter. Their winter clusters eat a lot and need fall or spring feeding by the beekeeper more than northern strains, but begin raising brood in midwinter and grow to produce record amounts of honey from good forage.

Only a colony of Northern American-bred and -fed Italians can turn out 300-plus pounds of surplus honey in supers stacked ten high. Original strains tried in North Europe failed to survive severe winters, but winter hardiness is now bred into North American stock. Gentle enough, these bees swarm excessively only if you let them get crowded. They are more inclined to rob than other strains. Modern Italians build colony strength reasonably fast, are unexcelled wax and honey producers, and are as predictable as any bee known. They have dusky brown to bright sun-yellow bands on their abdomens and many consider them the prettiest bees. Queens tend to lack black bands; some are almost all brownish-yellow and are easier to see on the frames than the dark strains.

Carniolans

A. m. carnica Pollmann, the Alpine bee, is native to the Austrian/Yugoslavian Alps where winters are long and severe, springs short, and summers hot. The Carniolans are becoming the standard breed throughout Northern Europe due to fast spring buildup, which starts slowly in a small brood nest, but accelerates dramatically when sufficient pollen is available. This bee swarms easily, however. Since this was the only way colonies could be multiplied before movable frames, it was considered a desirable trait. This gray-brown bee has a long tongue, so is good where red clover is a major nectar source. Very gentle, it can be kept in heavily populated areas. It is less inclined than most bees to run in panic on the combs when exposed to light.

The colony strength reduces rapidly in fall to a small cluster which nonetheless winters exceptionally well. In North America, Carniolans are strictly a hobby beekeeper's strain requiring considerable attention to prevent overcrowding and excessive swarming. Its negligible propolis use and rapid buildup make Carniolans a good strain for comb honey production for those with the time and patience to manage intensively.

Caucasians

A. m. caucasica. Gorb. is another gray to black, long-tongued bee from a strain that evolved in the high, cool mountain valleys of the Caucasus Mountains between the Black and Caspian Seas where Russia, Iran, and Turkey meet. Generally considered the gentlest strain of bees, Caucasians are often recommended as best for the novice. However, they are great builders of burr and brace comb and can be tremendous propolizers—glopping up comb with sticky, tarry-tasting "bee glue." If you plan to use your honey comb and all, and that is easiest for beginners, Caucasians may foul it with propolis. They are deliberate strength-builders, reaching peak numbers in mid-summer, well past the swarming season, so are a good strain for warmer climates. The total honey output may be less than with a strong Italian colony, but managing Caucasians is easier. They are placid. They build their own winter entrance reducer of propolized comb, a side-to-side, top-to-bottom barrier with a one or a series of bee-hole tunnels bored through. Interesting, but more than the usual nuisance to clean off come spring.

Brown Bee

A. m. mellifera L. is the old German brown or black bee that was a global standard until the early part of this century. Relatively large, the brown bee is short-tongued, nervous on the comb, and a creature of ocean-moderated climates, thus a slow spring starter. It was well suited to collecting the thick, wild heather honey, the production of which is greatly diminished in agricultural areas of Europe, but proved highly susceptible to disease. The brown bee is not as productive, manageable, or hardy as other strains, and you wouldn't want to buy this one if you could. Some brown bee strains continue to be kept, and they exist in the wild throughout the world. They are also used in hybridizing.

Crosses and Hybrids

Breeders are continually making and remaking crosses in an attempt to produce the perfect bee, one that is industrious, gentle, and calm on the comb but sufficiently protective of nest and honey, easy on winter stores but winter-hardy. All are claimed to be better in all respects than ordinary bees. The only problem is maintaining purity of the strain; frequent requeening is necessary. If you order any of these queens, have them marked for easy identification, wing-clipped to eliminate swarming flight by the queen, or both.

Among the best known:

Buckfast Queens. Native English brown bees were crossed with Italians, and used by the famous beekeeper Brother Adam and confreres of Buckfast Abbey to save the British bee industry from acarine disease in the early decades of this century. This vari-colored bee was bred for superior honey production, gentleness, a compact brood nest, and good wintering on limited stores. Try a bit of history; their sale is licensed in the U.S.A. only to Weaver Apiaries, Inc. of Navasota, Texas. Brother Adam's order gets a royalty on each queen, as well it should.

Mraz Queens. *Gleanings in Bee Culture* columnist Charles Mraz of Middlebury, Vermont, found his ideal bee by reselecting from Italian stock in the 1920s and crossing with other strains. Through a double selection process each year, the strain is main-tained and sold by several apiaries.

Hybrids, bred in a procedure originated by the USDA a genera-tion ago, exhibit hybrid vigor with accented good qualities. But, if the hybrid queen fails and is superseded (replaced by a new queen raised by the workers from hybrid eggs), the new queen will not ex-hibit those desirable hybrid characteristics, and may turn hostile or unproductive.

Dadant and Sons maintains its own hybridization program, of-fering two lines under its own name and through cooperating breeders such as the York Apiary, Jesup, Georgia. Hybri-Bees, Inc, licenses breeders such as Howard Weaver & Sons of Navasota, Texas, to produce its version of the hybrids. **Starline** is the Italian hy-brid, and some feel it is as close to Superbee as they've come. **Mid-nites**, hybridized from the gentle and slow-developing Caucasian strain as a beginner's bee, are found to be positively lethargic by some.

Italians Best Choice

Beginners are advised to stick with the manageable and produc-tive Italians. Nearly all wild honeybee colonies in North America are the Italian strain. In time, all colonies will supersede their queen, or your colony will swarm, led by your original queen. The new virgin queens will breed with local drones. Keeping Italians, you should have few problems. If you have a non-Italian queen, her offspring will be natural crosses which may be less manageable than the origi-nal strain. The only cure is to kill the old queen and replace her to reestablish your pure strain. You must requeen whether or not you have the time and patience and cash for a new queen.

Even finding non-Italian queens in the colony takes experience. And don't rely fully on marking the queen with paint or a sticker. It will help with early queen checks, but experience shows that half of all colonies supersede their queens each year, usually unbeknownst to the beekeeper. A marked queen has a 50 percent probability of never being seen after a few months in the nest. And, some beekeepers feel that the marking itself makes a queen less acceptable to the colony.

BUILDING THE HIVES

Your KD hives, frames, and equipment will come with illustrated assembly instructions that show how the parts fit together, but don't tell how to assemble them. An experienced woodworker will have few problems, but I'll assume that you are as much a klutz with hammer and nails as I was when I put my first hive together upside down and frames backwards.

First, on a sturdy worktable that won't mind a few scars, assemble your tools:

- **Large claw hammer**
- **Small tack hammer**
- **Sharp, sturdy-spined penknife**
- **Your hive tool, for a prybar and nail puller**
- **A wooden mallet or a soft-faced hammer or a block of wood to soften blows and prevent dents on the hive bodies**
- **An electric or egg-beater hand drill and small bits, $\frac{1}{16}''$ or so to make nail holes in thin or twisty-grained wood**
- **High-quality, water-resistant, slow-setting wood glue (resorcinol-based boat-builder's glue is best)**
- **A right angle. A small carpenter's angle is best but the cardboard back off a tablet of paper will do.**
- **Brad driver**
- **Nails if not supplied:**
  —$\frac{3}{4}''$ for putting foundation wedges in frames
  —$1\frac{1}{4}''$ for assembling the frames
  —$1\frac{3}{8}''$ galvanized for hive bodies
  —$2\frac{1}{4}''$ galvanized for hive bodies

1. Apply glue to the hive body joints.

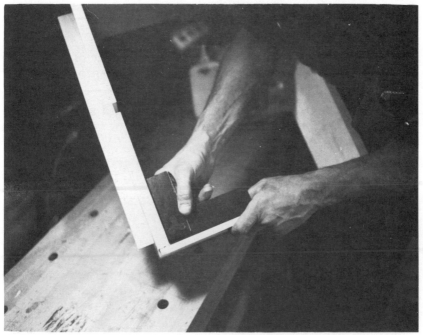

2. Use a carpenter's square to make certain that each hive body is square.

3. Use a wood block to soften hammer blows when snugging sticky finger joints together.

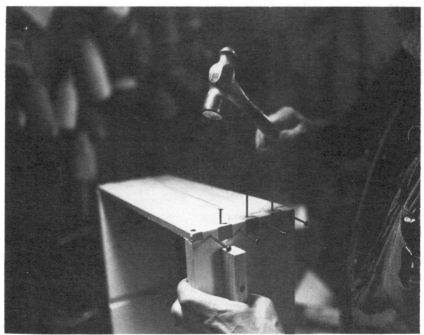

4. Hammer nails through drilled holes. If your hive bodies are not drilled, drill $\frac{1}{16}$" holes before nailing to avoid splitting the finger joints.

Completing the Hive Body

Hive bodies are first. The sides have finger joints that fit together, one over another. If nail holes aren't drilled in the jutting fingers of each side, drill them, right through the center of each finger. The thin top rail on some designs is especially prone to splitting.

To avoid bruising the wood, use a hardwood maul or soft-faced hammer, or put a wood block between a conventional hammer and the wood to knock the joints together. Try the fit of each joint before gluing. You may find that the joints fit too snugly. Little splinters of wood may even snap off if you force a fit. If you are a perfectionist and have the time, use a flat file to work the joints until the fit is smooth and the boards fit like fingers in a deerskin glove. It's a lot easier just to tap the joints gently until they fit, even if it does dent the wood a bit.

Apply glue to the inner surfaces of each joint, let it sit for a few minutes to get tacky, then fit the adjoining pieces together, long side piece to short end. **Be sure the milled-in hand holds face the same way on the boards or your hive body will be half upside-down**.

The edges of the joints won't be smooth, and glue will ooze out of the cracks. I wipe off most of the glue out of habit, but the bees won't notice if you don't.

When the glued pieces fit and all joints are snugged up, use the square to be sure all four corners are a true 90°. If one is right, the others will be too if all joints are tight. Then hammer a 1¼" galvanized nail in the thin top rail and 2 ¼" galvanized nails in the rest of the hive, going around tapping them in gradually, nail to nail and from joint to joint, reapplying the square as you go. Be sure the base of the box remains flat and square to the table as you nail, so it will sit level on the bottom board and support added hive bodies without any draft-inducing cracks between.

Using small nails, nail the metal frame rests into the rabbet cut out from the sides of the hive bodies.

Covers

Telescoping covers and inner covers are simple—four grooved or inletted sides and a fiberboard or plywood sheet to be nailed and glued together. The plywood makes a far sturdier top. The only trick is getting the metal cover of the telescoping cover to fit. Try gluing the wood and fitting the metal top before you nail the wood up. You may have to hammer out a corner or one bent side to get the metal to fit. Take care in nailing the metal. The nails can get misdirected easily in the thin wood rails.

Bottom Board

Bottom boards are even more simple than tops. The tongue-and-groove boards fit readily into grooved side rails, with a cleat at the rear end of the board. The entrance reducer fits on the front of this board, held in place snugly between the bottom board and the hive above it.

Hive Stand

Hive stands made from cypress are a bit tricky. I have not found any drilled for nails, and this twist-grained wood needs it. Use the square on the stands before driving any nails home, so the open rectangle will be square. Nail the back and two sides together first, then add the sloping entrance.

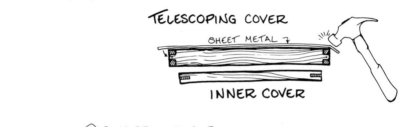

TELESCOPING COVER

SHEET METAL

INNER COVER

GLUE GROOVES BEFORE SPACING + NAILING SLATS

SLATTED RACK

HIVE STAND

Self-spacing Frames

Supering frames sold by most makers go together with no problem. The premium grade of brood frame by Root and others has a little point whittled into one (and only one) edge of the broad top end of the side members. This reduces the surface where one frame touches another, thus minimizing the amount of wood area the bees can gum up with propolis and burr comb. That's a big help when it is time to pry apart old brood frames after months in the nest.

1. A stout knife is helpful in splitting the wedge out of the top bar of each frame.

2. Glue applied, the side bar goes on the top bar.

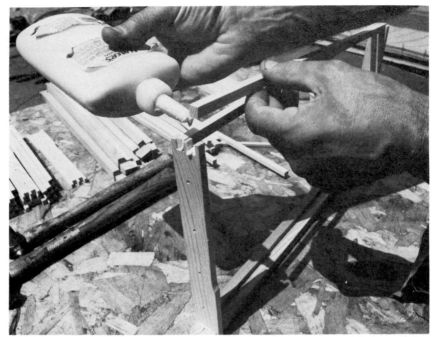

3. The two bottom bars are glued and snugged into the bottom of the side bars.

4. Then both top and bottom bars are nailed on.

5. With the reinforced beeswax foundation slipped into place, the wedge is nailed on.

6. Finally, the split support pins are pushed through the holes in the side bars.

When assembling these frames, keep the pointed edge aimed in the same direction on all frames. Conventionally, the point faces forward from the right side and backward on the left as you look down at the frame. Make all of yours the same, and make them sturdy. Frames are exposed to repeated prying and handling under a substantial load.

I glue frames for added strength, but you needn't if you don't want to bother. With glue, single 1¼" nails can be driven in from the sides. With no glue, put pairs of nails through both top and bottom bars and into the side members. Divided and grooved bottom bars are nailed up the same way.

INSTALLING
THE FOUNDATION

Inserting foundation takes patience and a bit of practice. It is floppy in any event and gets soft and hard to handle if you let it get warm.

Use a sharp knife to cut the wedge out of the top piece of the frame. Cut with the knife as close to the top of the kerf as you can get. If you just pop the wedge out, ridges of wood will remain in the kerf and the foundation won't fit well into the top bar. If a ridge does remain, cut it out.

Brood chamber foundation contains crimped wires that are bent in a 90° angle at one edge. Place this edge in the top bar kerf with the bent ends — little hooks — pointing out from the center. Turn the wedge bar with the cut edge out, milled side against the wax, and snug the top under the hooks. Press the wedge hard against the top bar, pinioning the wire hooks firmly, and nail it in with two of the smallest (¾") nails. Put the nails into the main body of the top bar, not as some instructions tell you into the thin rail opposite the cut-out wedge; it can split easily. Insert the nails at a sharp enough angle so that you don't dent the wax as you tap them home; leave the little head of each exposed for easy removal. A brad driver (about $5) makes this an easy task.

Insert the lower edge of the foundation in the groove in one-piece bottom rails or between split rails. Some instructions tell you to bow the center of the bottom rails up and put a nail through bottom bar and foundation to keep foundation taut. I've never done this, and find that the bees fasten the wax in good and tight on their own.

Finally, press support pins through all four holes in the side bars so the wax sheet fits neatly into the split end of each pin. You may find it easier to poke a nail through the holes in the end bars and enlarge them if pins go in with difficulty. If the fit is so tight that you must push hard, the pin can pop through suddenly and dent the wax.

When the hive is assembled, apply your choice of finish to wood that will be exposed to the weather, including all surfaces of the hive stand. Don't paint the frames or insides of boxes. Bees like plain wood. White exterior latex paint is conventional, easy to apply, and clean up after. Two coats will last for years.

Don't think you have to paint your hives white, though. The light, reflective coating does help reduce heat buildup if hives are to be set in full sun, and is to be recommended in a warm climate. In our locale, a light green is common, and it makes the hives less conspicuous in the fields. These days, I finish new beeware with a warm shade of brown stain. It doesn't show discoloration as easily as the white. More important, it absorbs heat rather than reflects as does a white finish. And on our mountain, there are more cold days when the bees can use added warmth than hot, sunny days when they might overheat.

Here's a stack of new hives ready for staining. I put on two coats of a good house stain, soaking the finger joints well. Note the three sizes of hive bodies. From the top, a ¾ size Western comb honey super with hand-hold cleats along two sides, a shallow super, a ¾ size super, and four full-size brood chambers.

Chapter 4

INTRODUCING
THE BEES

United Parcel and other commercial carriers won't handle bees, so if you buy yours direct from a shipper, they will come by mail. You will receive a postcard acknowledging the order and listing the week your bees will leave the apiary. A precise shipping date isn't feasible during the busy season, or fully reliable any time, as weather can delay things unexpectedly. Alert the post office, give your phone number, and arrange to pick up the bees during postal office hours the day they arrive.

Some suburban and country postal people are used to handling screened boxes containing a swarm of sweetly humming bees, but I've known in-town clerks to swallow real hard on seeing them for the first time. In the United States, bees sent Parcel Post, Special Handling, get passed along speedily by the postal corps and almost always arrive on the morning mail, 8:00 at our post office. Expect a phone call at 8:01.

Shipping Cage

The shipping cage has a rectangular frame about a foot long and half as deep with wooden top, bottom, and end pieces, and window screen forming the two large side panels. Top and ends may be plastered with shipping labels, state bee-health certificates, and installation instructions. Check the mailing date on the label. The cage contains a can of syrup to keep the swarm alive over the usual three-day shipping period and then some. But it doesn't offer luxury accommodations, and the bees will appreciate getting home for a cool drink.

Don't worry about a few dead bees. But if the bottom is solidly covered one bee thick and growing, get a signed voucher from the post office to that effect. If the apiary that supplies your bees does not guarantee live delivery, but insures the package, you'll have to file for the insurance and pay for another package. Shippers who guarantee live arrival will replace the bees if you send them the post office voucher by special delivery mail with a postal money order for shipping charges, an explanation, and your invoice number.

It is best to telephone the apiary for replacement instructions. Charging shipping costs to a credit card by phone is acceptable to the larger shippers and saves considerable time.

What's Inside

Inside the cage are a metal can filled with sugar syrup and a small cage containing the queen and three or more attendants, with both cage and can covered with a mass of bees that will be packed together if it's cool, arrayed against the screen and fanning loudly if it's hot. Hot bees make a considerable racket; cold bees remain immobile and murmuring to themselves until you jolt the cage, which makes them grumble. Drop the cage and they growl.

The sounds can be frightening at first. Just remember, the bees are operating under an artificially induced, but genuine swarming instinct. They are as gentle as bees will ever be. They have no nest to defend and no reason to sting. If the buzzing on a hot day is upsetting, spray them gently with tepid water and put them in a cool, dark cellar. They will calm down and pull together in a quiet cluster around the queen.

Check for Strangers

At the post office, inspect the outside of the package to be sure you haven't picked up any local bees attracted by the odor of the cluster. Workers drift between colonies all the time. This does no harm unless they are carrying disease. But you don't want to squash one in picking up the cage, and get your first sting from an innocent

The queen cage hangs from the top of the shipping cage next to the syrup can, which is covered with bees. This queen cage hangs by a screen strip and comes out with the syrup can.

In this cage, the queen cage comes out separately from the syrup can. You can use the syrup brush to dust off a few bees hanging on.

visitor. Blow hard on the strangers or flick them off with your finger and they will go home.

Bees can squeeze through narrow cracks, so make sure the cage frame has not been sprung loose in transit and that the wood slats or staples holding the screen in place are secure. If not, hammer in a few small nails or staples before you begin manipulating the cage. The bees will stir to let you know they prefer that you hammer gently and take a little time between taps. Patience and slow motion are important in all phases of bee-handling. The predators that bees have evolved to dislike all move quickly — darting bee-eating bird beaks, batting bear claws, lapping skunk tongues, and the like. Move methodically and the bees will call you a friend.

A First Feeding

The main sustenance an adult worker bee needs during her brief lifetime is sucrose, obtained naturally from nectar or bee-keeper-provided from white granulated sugar, and pure water. Mix up a sugar syrup of equal parts of sugar and hot water, pouring the sugar into the water while stirring. Let it cool before giving it to the bees. Store unused sugar syrup in a cool place so it won't ferment.

Feed Through the Wire

To feed the bees, put the cage where spilled sugar water won't make a sticky mess, angle it over a little, and use a clean paintbrush to trickle syrup onto the wire and into both sides of the bee cluster. The bees will eagerly lick it off the wire and their own bodies. Feed them a cup or two, and don't mind any puddling on the cage bottom. They'll clean it up.

Listen well. The humming will subside and your bees will sound more contented as they feed. Volume will change with hive conditions, but the sweet and low tone of that contented sound is a delight to the beekeeper's ears. Try to memorize it.

Get Acquainted

Once they've had a cup or two of syrup, they'll be happy, and you can play around with them for a bit to get used to having bees in your life. A little familiarity will eliminate the fear we all have of stinging insects.

Pour a puddle of syrup through the screen onto the cage bottom and shake some bees into it. Just bang one end of the cage on a table and a festoon of hanging bees will fall — hissing a bit, but not for long. They get batted around on wind-blown flowers all the time and don't mind being jostled. Watch their little tongues go at the syrup. Touch the feet and antenna of bees crawling inside the cage

Paint warm sugar syrup on the sides of the shipping cage to welcome the new bees.

wire. They can't sting through the wire. Blow on the cluster and see what it does. Poke a broom straw through the wire and into the bees. Stir them gently. Fast movement will meet antagonism. Slow, gentle movement won't be noticed. You are learning two major skills of bee handling: do nothing until you feel safe—have a confidence born of know-how—and do everything in a slow, gentle, and deliberate manner.

INSTALLING
THE BEES

It is best to install the bees in late afternoon of the day they arrive. At dusk, their instinct is to head for shelter, and they'll more readily move into the new hive. Some beekeepers feel they can hive a swarm, wild or artificial, more easily on a cold and drizzly day. I find that bees are grumpy when the weather is unpleasant, and so delay installing them for a day or two.

Unless you are installing immediately, you should inspect the queen and offer her some liquid refreshment by way of welcome. She and her attendants come with an ample supply of bee candy, but if the trip has been hot, they may need water. Bang the cage gently on a firm surface until the bees fall to the cage floor. Shine a flashlight up at the queen cage, a rectangular wood block with two or three adjacent holes bored partly through one side, making a kind of open figure-eight opening that is covered with screening. The queen will be covered by her attendants and hard to see at several inches' distance and through two screens, but look for a bee that has a longer abdomen than the others. That's your new queen and mother of the colony-to-be. Trickle lukewarm water through the outer screen and into the queen cage and all over the inhabitants. They'll drink what they want and shake off the rest. If you must delay introducing the bees to the hive, feed the workers and give the queen and her attendants water at least once a day.

A Sting-proof Outfit

Further manipulations will release bees, albeit swarm-gentled bees, so don protective gear. Beekeepers' experience has proven that bees prefer their handlers to wear light-colored clothing. You may find they are happy in general but will buzz angrily and sting a red kerchief or black leather boot.

One summer I tried some nifty, new, grit-palmed plastic gloves for lifting full supers. The grip they offered was wonderful, but the smell of the glove material infuriated the bees. White cotton garments, fresh-laundered, sun-dried, and well-aired, are apparently liked best; smelly, old dark-colored fishing-type shirts the worst. Honey-loving bears have been robbing bees for a lot longer than man has, and I'd guess that bees react to any dark, moving object with a strong animal or non-bee odor.

So, dress to suit your new friends. Tuck the skirt of your bee veil into the buttoned-up collar of a shirt. Wear sleeves down to your wrists, cuffs buttoned, and gloves pulled up over them. Wear pants tucked into or cinched over and around the tallest boots you have. Bees love to crawl into dark places, and elastics around cuffs will provide a bee barrier to the tunnels into your shirtsleeves or pants.

TRANSFERRING THE BEES

Give the bees a more than generous feeding about a half-hour before moving them into their new home. A pint of warm syrup isn't too much. They don't have any instinctive need to act ornery, and a copious feeding will fill their nectar crops so full they couldn't sting if they wanted to. Also, a full belly will fuel their next strong instinctive behavior—to draw out the honeycomb in their new home.

Get Ready

Set the hive body which will be the colony's brood chamber on the bottom board and the permanent base. Put nine of the ten foundation-filled frames in the brood chamber (the little cage the queen is in will occupy the space where the tenth frame would go). Rest the two-part cover against the off-side of the beebox, ready to be installed.

Fill the jar of the Boardman feeder with 50:50 sugar water and have it ready to be installed under the front of the hive, in the long slot of the entrance reducer. Reducers and feeder bases from different suppliers aren't necessarily perfectly matched, so be sure there is a one- or two-bee wide entrance at one or both sides of the feeder base so the bees can get in and out one or two at a time. And try the reducer/feeder/hive match for size before it is filled with several thousand bees.

Collect your tools:

- **Hive tool**
- **Pliers**
- **Thin-bladed knife**
- **Small screwdriver or nail file (for prying staples)**
- **Bee brush**
- **Thumbtack and two small nails bent at a 90° angle (which you may need to attach the queen cage to the frames).**

Arrange the tools in a pocket or belt so that you can reach them without looking.

Steps in Opening the Cage

You are about to open a cage filled with thousands of bees, and it will probably be the most nervous-making step in your beekeeping career. Here are the steps you will go through; we'll discuss some details a bit later. It's a good idea to study the photos and get the sequence of steps firmly in mind. Be advised, though, that the cage arrangement pictured is just one of several you may encounter. The principles are the same for all, though. And remember, these are pacified bees. Take your time and move slowly and deliberately.

1. Remove the thin wood cover nailed to the top of the cage. It holds in the queen's cage and the syrup can, on which the bees are clustered. With the hive tool, pry up each end of the cover and then tap it back down. This will expose the heads of the nails and you can pull them out with pliers. Leave the cover in place for now.

2. Holding the cover on with your thumbs, bang the cage on the ground. The bees will cascade to the bottom of the cage with a gentle hum. You've probably given them so much syrup they are too full and contented to protest very much. Remove the wooden cover. You'll see the top of the can in a round cutout. The queen cage may be in a keyhole-shaped cutout next to the can and held on by a metal disc, or attached by a screen strap, or not apparent at all. A few bees may try to squeeze out around the can, but don't pay any attention to them. Remember, the bees don't have a home and young bees to protect and they don't have any reason to sting. All they want is to get into your new hive and begin drawing comb.

3. Tip the cage over and slide the syrup cage and queen cage out. They'll slip right into your hand, though you may have to re-move a staple or small nail to remove the queen cage. Replace the cover on the shipping cage, gently brush any bees off the outside of the queen cage, and take it aside for a good examination. The queen, with her longer, more pointed abdomen, should be obvious among the workers milling around her. Note the white candy plug filling one end of the cage. There's a little cork in the wood at the end of the cage.

Step 1.

Step 3.

Step 4.

Step 6.

Step 7.

Step 8.

4. Use your knife or screwdriver to pry the cork out of the candy end of the queen cage so the bees can gnaw out the candy plug to free the queen. If you see little bee eyes, not candy, when you remove the cork you have the wrong end of the cage. Replace that cork and pull the cork at the opposite end.

5. Use the thumbtack or bent nails as needed to suspend the queen cage, candy side up, between two frames in the center of the bee box so it will be directly under the cutout in the inner cover (so the queen cage can be easily inspected and removed later). Be sure the screen sides of the little cage face out into the hive, not up against the frames, so the package bees can communicate with the queen through the screen and air can circulate around her while she is being gnawed free.

6. Gently shake the bees out over the frame tops. You may find they ball up and roll on the cage bottom, and they may grumble as they are shaken but their tone will immediately improve in pitch as they sense the foundation below. They'll begin to flow down between the frames, eager to get to work.

7. Wait until the bees are well down on the foundation; then slide on the inner cover. In our cold climate I always cover the cut-out opening over a new colony with a piece of thin shingle or the cover from the shipping cage and leave it there until it is time to install supers. This conserves the 90° + heat the queen needs to lay and workers need to soften comb to draw it into wax. With the cut-out left open, I'd be afraid that the relatively small package bee colony would have to cluster just as they did in the shipping cage to keep the queen warm in cool weather, and no hive work would get done. Put on the outer cover.

8. Lean the shipping cage against the front of the hive so any bees that were more interested in cleaning up your syrup feedings than going to work in the hive can leave at their convenience. They'll find their way inside in short order.

9. And, with the entrance reducer and Boardman entrance feeder in place, you're done.

Don't Drop the Queen

Instructions printed on some cages can be misinterpreted by a nervous novice. They tell you to remove the little keeper on the queen cage. Well, if you cut or pry the keeper off before extracting the queen cage from the package, the queen and associates will fall into the main clump of bees, causing a short, angry-sounding buzz. I know—it happened to me the first time. Then, hands shaking, you'll have to pull out the feed can and fish the queen cage from the seething mass as a thousand bees fly out into your face (happy to be free and uninterested in stinging, but you won't believe it at the time). Smoke will just confuse things, as the bees have no frames to hide in and no comb from which to take honey, so don't use your smoker. Be sure the queen cage is out and in your hands before you remove anything other than the original wood cover and the syrup can.

VARIATIONS ON INTRODUCTION

I like to hold the bees until weather is fine, and then shake them out slowly, permitting the bees to flow down around the suspended queen cage into a hive almost filled with nine frames. The package can't begin to cover that many frames, of course, and many experts remove half of the frames, install the queen cage between two frames, then shake the bees quickly into the bottom of the hive. Or, you can install the queen and just put the shipping cage in the hive, top opening up; when you close up the bees will quickly move out and around the queen. Still another way is to install the queen, put an empty super on top of the brood chamber, and invert the shipping cage on top of the frames, with the syrup can hole right over the queen cage. If you are in a hurry or if the weather is unpleasant, these options may fit. In any event, if the weather is downright cold, be sure to shake some bees on top of the queen cage so she won't catch a chill.

If you've ordered a race of bees other than Italians, you may notice a difference in size and coloring between the queen and the package workers. Carniolans, Caucasians, and hybrid queens are normally shipped with packages of the more common Italians. You haven't been cheated. The Italians will serve their new queen, no matter her parentage. The size and coloring difference in the early weeks make it easier to spot the queen in your early checks of her productivity. And the colony will change characteristics over the coming month as the new queen's progeny hatch and the package bees die out, mission accomplished.

Let Them Get Acquainted

Don't be tempted to release your queen directly into the mass of package bees. She is not mother to them, and they have not lived surrounded by the sophisticated and biologically active chemical scents (pheromones) that a queen uses to regulate activity in the colony. If you just dumped the queen among them, the bees might sense that she is a stranger, and kill her by "balling," surrounding her until she starves or suffocates. Introducing a queen to a new colony with a candy-plugged queen cage may seem to be an overly laborious procedure, but it has been time-proven for generations. While the queen is being gnawed free, she is constantly serviced by the package bees. By the time she is released, her pheromones will be spread throughout the colony and she will be accepted.

Tricky Queen Cages

Different bee shippers use different styles of queen cages. All have a candy plug to slow the introduction process and all contain little cork plugs at the ends. But there are several attachment variations. You won't know until you open it what type you'll find beneath your shipping cage cover. Here are the most common types and how to suspend them between a pair of adjoining frames.

1. A cage with a small metal disk already nailed to its top can be suspended from between the frames by the disk.

2. A cage with a strip of screening attached can be stuck on with a thumbtack.

3. A cage lacking any attachments at all can be suspended by two bent nails. Use pliers to press the pointed tips into the candy plug end of the cage so the bent-over tops protrude from each side like little ears to hang the cage from adjoining frames.

A Final Check

Before you count yourself done, make one double check of your handiwork. Remove the covers and make certain the cutout in the center of the inner cover is directly over the queen cage. If it isn't, move the cage. In a few days, when you check to be sure the queen is free, you can take a quick peek without removing the inner cover and disturbing the bees.

Now, put the covers back on the hive, flick any curious bees off your clothes and veil, move away slowly, take a deep breath, and you are done.

And please accept my congratulations. The bees are installed, they're happily building their first comb, and you're a genuine beekeeper. Welcome to a gentle confraternity.

You've opened the package of bees and taken out the queen cage. You look in, identify the queen—and she's dead.

This doesn't happen often, but it can. What do you do?

First, nail the cover back on the package. Put it in a cool spot, such as a cellar.

Second, call your supplier, and ask him to speed you another queen.

While waiting for the queen, feed the bees twice daily.

When the queen arrives, install the bees.

Bee Toilet Habits

As you unload the package, some bees will fly around. Not yet oriented to the new hive location, a few will expel surprisingly large drops of a light yellow-brown liquid that will dry quickly into a glue-like "yellow rain" wherever they happen to fall. This isn't the disorder dysentery, but normal bee elimination. Bees can hold it for a very long time, months, in fact, until half their body weight consists of excreta. Your bees won't continue soiling the home area for long, but will fly out into the area immediately in front of the hive.

In discussing hive location earlier, I mentioned that every worker bee in the colony will take cleansing flights during winter warm spells. Think of a winter cluster of some 20,000 bees spotting the neighbor's laundry. It isn't too late to move the hive to any spot you choose, but do it now before your flying bees become oriented to the hive, using trees and other landmarks and memorizing for life the nest's location. If you wait too long, you'll have to take the bees to unfamiliar territory requiring a new orientation, and leave them there for a week or so before bringing them back. Bees moved just a short distance will return to the old hive location and will drift away to any colony that strikes their fancy.

If You Are Stung

If you get zapped, don't slap at the bee. Your fast hand motion and the banana-smelling pheromone left by the stinging bee can bring more bees down on you. If your smoker is fired up, puff the stung place to mask the scent. The bee that got you can't do further damage—indeed, she will die shortly. As she pulled away, she left her stinger and attached pump and venom reservoir imbedded, but alive and steadily forcing more poison into your hide.

Scrape out the stinger with a fingernail or the hive tool. Don't grab and pull, but scrape where the stinger enters your skin. Squeezing the little sack that the bee abandoned along with the stinger will force more venom in and make the sting worse.

It's Done

Even if you were stung, congratulate yourself on your first success with bees. The first time is the worst. They didn't come roaring out in a mini-tornado like in an old cartoon, did they? Actually, they are kind of cute, crawling around nosing your clothes, huh? I bet you fall in love with them once your heartbeat slows down. And, if you're like me, you'll spend hours sitting in the sun watching the bees come and go. There's a fascination to it. They are funny little things as they tumble over one another at the entrance. The big, bumbling drones that can fly bullet-fast in the mating area are especially clumsy as they come home to crib a meal. Look at the huge eyes that almost meet on top of their heads—the better to spot flying queens, I presume. You can pick up a drone. They have no stingers. If one pops audibly, seeming to explode into your hand, it's a sign of affection, I guess. That's a drone's mating response, and, like a worker that has just stung, he will sacrifice his life in this one act. If you have a microscope, get out a slide and some blue stain and look at the several million bee sperm the drone has expelled. You might also pick a dead bee from in front of the hive and look at the compound eyes, mouth parts, and all, under low power.

FOLLOW UP

Give the bees three to five days to free the queen and get used to their new home. Keep the syrup jar topped up. Even if a full-blown spring honeyflow is on, the new colony lacks enough older foraging workers to bring in nectar enough to fuel hive-building activity. A quart a day is a typical syrup consumption rate for a three-pound package.

On the third day, if it is warm, dry, and not windy, don head net and gloves and look in the hive to make certain that the queen has been freed. Remove the outer cover, then look down through the cut-out in the inner cover. If the candy plug is gone from the queen cage, the queen is free, even though the queen cage is filled with milling bees. If the candy plug is still intact, shove a nail through it until you have made a tunnel the bees can enlarge quickly. Careful – don't hit the queen. Check daily until the candy plug is gone and the queen is released.

If the weather is poor, leave the queen cage in place, close the hive, and wait two weeks until it's time to check the queen's laying pattern. If you disturb the hive in bad weather this early, the bees may get a wrong signal and kill the queen.

If the weather is fine and plenty of flowers are blooming in the neighborhood, the bees coming and going in a purposeful manner, you can pull the inner cover and remove the queen cage, then put in that tenth frame. Push all the other frames together so there's room for that tenth one at one end of the hive. You'll want your smoker for this job, so it's time to learn how to use it.

Firing Up the Smoker

Facile manipulation of the smoker is the skill that separates bee-keepers from lesser folk. You can fuel the smoker with anything that will smolder. Old rags and wet hay are frequently recommended, but they smell awful, and I don't like smoking my bees with anything I find unpleasant. Feed sacking is the smoker fuel usually recommended in old publications, and it does ignite and smolder readily. But these days our livestock feed comes in sacks made of plastic fabric. We can still get seed grain and potatoes in traditional burlap, but much of it is still made from hemp fiber which comes from the infamous Asiatic pot herb Cannabis sativa. Not wanting my bees flying funny, I fuel my smoker with sweet birch or hickory shavings from the woodpile.

Twist a bit of newspaper into a loose spike, light the bottom, and stuff it in the smoker body. As the paper blazes, add thin wood slivers or whittling splints a few at a time until there is a good wood fire going. Keep stuffing in fuel to keep it from blazing too brightly. When the smoker is full, close it – using gloves, as the smoker will be hot. Puff the bellows to fan the fire and expel smoke.

The idea is to establish a bed of coals at the bottom of the smoker, stuff fuel on top as needed, and supply sufficient oxygen at the bottom with the bellows to keep a smoldering fire going. Use the bellows to maintain the fire even when you aren't smoking bees. Only experience can teach you how to run your own combination of smoker, fuel supply, and pyrotechnic instinct.

Bees are affected primarily by the smell, not by visible particulates in the smoke, and too much heat can make them run in fear. You want a steady stream of cool smoke, not a great billowing cloud or a puny little bit. Too much smoke will make the bees want to fly; too little will antagonize them. Just the right amount sends them scurrying to the comb to gorge on honey, which pacifies them further. Only experience or observing an experienced beekeeper can teach the right touch.

WHY BEES REACT TO SMOKE

I speculate that bees' reaction to smoke, running to the honey and gorging, evolved over fifty million years' coexistence with fires. Evolutionarily successful bee colonies stoked up on food preparatory to fleeing before the fire got close enough to pose danger. Then, if fire did threaten the colony, they'd fly off and return when flames had passed, to salvage what they could. Even melted comb in a charred tree can be returned to use. I use the smoker as if it simulates the effect of a distant, but approaching brushfire.

Firing up a new stainless steel, jumbo-size bee smoker.

Two weeks have passed since you installed the bees and their queen. It's time to check the laying pattern of the queen, the work of the worker bees, and, if you haven't been able to do this before, to take out the queen cage and put in the tenth frame.

Open your hive on a warm, sunny day when plenty of flowers are blooming. It's not always possible, I know. But on cool and overcast days, nectar and pollen aren't coming in fast enough to keep the bees from feeling grumpy.

Put on protective gear and go to the hive with the smoker going. Approach the hive from the rear or either side, but not the front, where you'll be in the bees' line of flight.

Force three puffs of smoke at the entrance, holding the smoker a foot or more away from the entrance. This smoke should calm the guard bees on duty just inside. Wait a minute. Remove the outer cover and set it aside.

The inner cover won't be propolized to the hive body yet, so should be easy to remove. Lift one side of it slowly, then puff in some smoke. You should hear a low HHHUUUMMMmmmmmmmm as the bees comment on the sudden exposure to light. Some beekeepers feel the light pacifies the bees. I'm not sure that I agree, so have the smoker aimed and ready. Lift off the inner cover.

If conditions are good, the bees may ignore you and continue working the frames. They may be lined up along the frame tops, chewing away at the comb. But if they poke their heads above the frame tops, antenna and little eyes all peering at you, they need smoking. Keeping the smoker a foot or more away, lay a stream of smoke along the frame tops until the bees abandon the top inch of foundation. The volume and pitch of their humming may increase, but it will not sound threatening.

You will quickly learn to gauge a colony's mood by its hum. A contented colony makes a sound that varies in intensity, but remains in a low frequency range that is pleasant and soothing to human ears, a happy sound appropriate to a warm spring day with fruit trees in bloom. After the opening hum, an unsmoked and happy colony will sound content, and bees that fly up to inspect you will buzz around slowly, acting curious rather than hostile so long as your movements are deliberate. If several bees come out flying straight and fast to check you, stand still until they depart. Smoke them if they land on you. Alarm a single bee and it can signal the colony that danger's afoot.

Remove the Queen Cage

Once the bees have settled down, you can pry the queen cage out of the light yellow brood comb the bees have built around it. Lay it on the frames, and bees milling inside the queen cage will exit quickly. Look down between the frames. See any white bulges? That's new-drawn comb filled with new honey, the watery syrup you provided already masticated and fanned by the bees down to 17 percent moisture that turns nectar to honey. It's already stored and capped with pristine white wax. (For the record, this doesn't qualify as salable honey. Only pure nectar-based honey does. It's every bit as good for the bees, though, and that's what counts just now.)

Just below the honey will be a thin arc of pollen waiting to be fed to developing brood. And below that the queen will be peering into successive cells, then inserting her abdomen to deposit a single gleaming white egg in each. Her laying pattern is a series of concentric half-circles and the developing larvae are . . . but you have two weeks to wait before seeing that little miracle. Disturbing the nest this early could cause the new colony to kill the queen. For now, scrape any broken comb from where the queen cage was waxed to the frame tops, and use the hive tool to push the frames together from one side of the box, closing the space the queen cage occupied. Push slowly and gently so the bees on the frames below can get out of the way. In particular, you don't want to crush the queen. Put the tenth frame at the end of the hive and close up.

READING THE MOOD OF THE BEES

Put an ear to the hive body before you check a colony. The locus and intensity of sound compared with season and weather conditions will tell you what is going on inside. Silence on a cool day means the bees are clustering to conserve warmth. Silence combined with lessened activity at the entrance on a good flying day may signify trouble. A hearty hum means that comb is being drawn or brood tended. A gentle roar in the brood chamber comes from hive ventilation or housekeeping; from a super it means that honey is being evaporated.

The hum you hear on opening a hive always sounds a little anxious for a bit, louder and at a higher vibration rate and tone than normal. If it doesn't change to a contented tone immediately, the bees are grumpy. If it rises in tone and volume, they may be downright angry. They will crawl up to the frame tops and peer, and flying bees will circle rapidly and dart into your face. This is a warning: "Keep off our turf." Random stinging may begin if you persist. Professional beekeepers with work to do ignore the threats and use a lot of smoke. I perform essential chores and quit early. If your bees remain alarmed after the first opening, puff smoke liberally under the cover and wait a bit. Remove the cover, smoke the frames liberally, do what work you must, and close up.

With the smoker going and the first frame removed, I check the brood. When I'm inspecting later in the year, I will lay the covers on the ground as a base to place hive bodies that I remove.

A hostile colony will warn you in unmistakable terms. The hum becomes loud, shrill and strident, a high-pitched beeeeeeeeeeeeee sound—possibly where they got their name in the old days; our word is from Old English *beo*, or *bia* in Old (High) German. The vibration rate is unpleasant bordering on fearsome to humans, high enough to cause inner ear discomfort in many animals. It is an adrenalin-generating alarm signal that strikes a primordial chord in humans, the same as a rattlesnake's burrrrr or a dog's grrrrr or an infant's high keening wail. Bees usually will give you enough time to think better, to close up and return another day. But they may not; they may emerge en masse, stinging in considerable numbers. Applying constant smoke will help, but bees will still fly around rapidly and at high buzz, trying to sting. You are best advised to retreat and try again on the next warm and sunny day.

Weather and nectar flow are not the only arbiters of bee's temperament. Lack of a satisfactory queen, disease, excess moisture, pests, and predators can all set them off. You'll encounter most of these problems over time. A strain may also become nasty through hybridization as a queen is superseded. These are seldom problems with a new package colony. Gauge your visits to the weather, keep the bees supplied with syrup, and your first few visits with the bees will be delightful.

Chapter 5

EARLY SPRING
MANAGEMENT

Your package bees are an artificially produced swarm, but they exhibit full and genuine swarm behavior. For the first few weeks, their prime instinct is to draw comb and to raise the young bees that will go out and gather the honey to see them through the winter (or to throw another swarm if conditions in the new hive aren't satisfactory). Even the older bees, those three weeks or more from hatching who would normally be engaged in foraging, will pitch in. Bees will hang in festoons, producing wax from glands on their abdomens. Others will chew it and the foundation into worker-rearing cells so rapidly the queen can get down to serious laying practically from the day she is freed.

Life Cycle

The eggs will hatch in three days. The younger of the package bees will feed the grub-like larvae for six more days, then apply a wax cap to their cells where they will pupate and spin a cocoon. There they will metamorphose, then gnaw their way out twenty-one days after the eggs were laid. They're now young adult worker bees.

Like the juvenile package bees that tended them, these new young spend the first three weeks of life doing house chores: successively cleaning out brood cells, feeding larvae, building comb, then ventilating the hive, and finally serving as guards. In their fourth week they earn their wings and move out of the hive to become foragers after nectar and pollen, water, or propolis for another three weeks or so, when they wear out, and sweetly pass on to wherever the really good workers in this life go.

You probably won't notice it, but the colony's flying population will diminish gradually over the first six weeks as the package bees die off naturally, but before your own queen's offspring are old enough to fly. Then, after the sixth week, there will be a population explosion.

Continue to Feed

I continue to supply syrup until all the brood chamber comb is drawn, even if I'm refilling the feeder into early summer. This assures the bees of adequate food to build comb and raise the young, but also encourages them to load the outer frames of the brood chamber with sugar-based honey so they will want to—no, have to—expand into the supers, come the major nectar flows. The honey will also serve as a larder for the periods in summer and fall when nectar stops unbeknownst to the beekeeper, and when large colonies need a great deal of energy just to keep body and brood going.

The syrup will be consumed quickly on warm, good-flying days, but almost ignored if the air gets chilly and the bees cluster to keep the queen and brood warm. Syrup can ferment in warm weather, so don't let any remain unconsumed for more than a day or two. Scrub the jar with soap and hot water when the first little, round jelly blobs of gray or green sugar mold begin to show inside on the glass.

Keep Them Cool

Very Important: The bees will keep themselves warm, but you must not let them overheat. A reduced entrance can restrict their ability to ventilate the hive, brood can die, and wax melt. Especially for hives in full sun, if heat and humidity rise in unspringlike fashion, say temperatures hit the eighties when they are normally in the sixties, enlarge the entrance during the day (at least) until things cool down.

On good days, the mature bees will go foraging. Look for the pollen gatherers returning with their **corbicula**, the little baskets on their rear legs, filled with varicolored balls of pollen. If a good number of bees – never the majority, but one out of four or six – is **not** bringing in pollen, you can assume that the local forage or the weather isn't cooperating. You should supply a substitute to go along with the sugar syrup or the colony may not have sufficient protein to produce new bees.

ARTIFICIAL POLLENS

An artificial pollen formula developed by the USDA's Beltsville, Maryland, research labs provides 13 percent protein and 70 percent carbohydrate from augmented soy flour. It is mixed with sugar syrup and sold commercially as Beltsville Bee Diet.

I make a pollen substitute from ingredients available at any health food store. Mix three parts by weight soyflour with one part of brewer's yeast for a basic dry feed. Some beepeople add up to one part nonfat dry milk. Mix in as much natural pollen as you have for better acceptance by the bees; even a small amount will make the artificial product more attractive to them. *Do not* use purchased bee pollen; you have no way of knowing where it came from. None of it is checked for bee disease, and imported pollen has been a proven carrier of the disease nosema.

You may find wild pollen in harvestable quantities in a cattail swamp, but not until well after the critical early spring weeks are past. To save some for next year, bang ripe cattail heads against the side of a garbage can with a plastic bag in it. Winnow out the cattail frass and freeze the pollen.

Feeding Dry Mix

Feed the dry mix by sprinkling it on frame tops or putting it in a cigar box with half-inch holes drilled in all four sides. Sprinkle some on the box top and leave it near the hives. The bees will find it. An easily handled pollen cake can be made by mixing the dry ingredients with enough 2:1 sugar-water syrup to bind a patty into a hamburger-like consistency, size, and shape. Do not mix with honey from any outside source unless you boil a 1:2 water/honey mix for five minutes; even store-bought eating honey can carry disease spores. Keep a supply of patties on frame tops until you see the bees carrying natural pollen.

Visiting the Hive

From the beginning, plan to make at least one non-intrusive quick check per week to follow each colony's growth, prevent excessive crowding, and preclude swarming if you can. Swarming requires new queens, and queens take sixteen days to develop from an egg. That once-a-week check should give you plenty of time to service the bees as needed.

Open the hive and disturb the bees as infrequently and as briefly as possible. If you can possibly help it, never perform a major operation, especially on a new or weak colony, when the temperature is much below 70° F. The bees must maintain a temperature of 93° to 95° around the brood. Open the top and out rushes the heat. The hive will lose vital energy and the bees must consume more honey to warm the queen and the brood. During those first few weeks, it is hard to resist opening the hive every fine afternoon, but you should do most of your observing from outside the hive. A real beekeeper learns to gauge much about the bees' condition from outside the hive, and that takes time spent quietly observing.

FIRST CHECK OF THE QUEEN

After ten days to no more than two weeks, make your first full-scale hive inspection to check the queen's productivity. Pick a warm and sunny day, dress well, and fire up the smoker. You'll be removing frames covered with bees, so you may have to use the smoker more freely than when you opened the hive briefly to remove the queen cage and add the tenth frame.

Smoke the entrance and remove the telescoping cover. Set the cover upside down to one side where it is handy but not in the way. Now smoke under the inner cover. Wait a half-minute or so and remove it. Check the bees on the inner cover. If the queen is among them, replace the covers and come back later.

The inner cover can go atop the telescoping cover. (And, later in the year you can use the covers as a place to stack hive bodies. If you stack them all at an angle to one another, you will crush fewer bees as you work.)

A Routine

Put the smoker at a convenient location. Mine has a hook and I keep it on the hive body to my left. Other beekeepers prefer to hold their smoker between their knees. Just have it handy so that any time you see more little bee eyes peering at you over the frame tops than bee bottoms working the comb, you can lay a few puffs of smoke over the hive. Keep the entrance smoked too.

It's good to establish a routine for hive inspections. First, remove the frame that is nearest you. Place the curved end of the hive tool between the tops of the first and second frames near the end bars. Twist gently. Repeat at the other end. Now you can pry up the ends of the first frame, or grab it with a frame lifter, and pull the first frame from the box. Remove it slowly so bees can get out of the way.

Lean the frame against the side of the hive, bottom bar on the ground and top bar resting against the hive body. Remember how you placed the frame against the hive so you can return it to its original position, not end-for-end. No need for the bees to waste time reestablishing precise bee space between the comb faces.

Now, with working space you can check the rest of the frames. Free the next frame with a gentle twist of the hive tool. Lift it out and hold it over the others for examination. When you've checked it, put it back in the space occupied by the first frame. Proceed through the frames, removing #3 and putting it back where frame #2 was, then frame #4 taking the place of #3 and so on. When you are done, you can move all the frames back to their proper locations by inserting the hive tool curved end between the hive side and frame #2 and twisting gently to push all nine frames back into position. Then slide the original frame back in its place.

Remove the Queen Cage

If you didn't have a chance to remove the queen cage before, do so now. You'll find the bees have been at work, trying to fill the more-than-beespace openings on each side of the little cage. They will begin to fill the space between the frames with bridge comb and often build brood or honey comb down from the cage itself. Just twist the two frames enough to dislodge the cage and remove it, comb and all.

Leave the cage on the frames a few minutes, and any bees hanging to it will scamper off. Shake off any remaining when you are ready to remove the cage and close the hive.

As you lift out the two frames nearest the cage, cut away the bridge comb with the sharpened end of your hive tool. Don't discard this wax near the hive, since it could attract robbers and pests.

Be careful when lifting the frames out of the hive. The queen may be laying eggs in the area, even in that comb hanging from the cage. If you spot her there, ease her gently onto the nearby frames.

If the weather has been at all good, half the frames should be drawn, at least in part. Usually they will be.

If a substantial amount of the frame foundation isn't drawn, the queen may not be producing the pheromones to inspire the workers, but that's rare. Unless your upcoming inspection indicates that her brood laying pattern is bad, blame it on the weather or nectar flow and give her another week or two. Disease or pest problems are rare this early, particularly if you are using new or fumigated equipment.

A BAD START

I had one package start off poorly. It was a dark Carniolan queen sent with three pounds of leather-colored Italians.

It was snowing when they arrived, and I installed them in a four-frame nuc inside the house and kept them cooped up there for two days. Once installed, nuc frames and all, in a new full-sized mail-order brood chamber, the bees never seemed to get buzzing, and after almost three weeks only the original four frames from the super were partly drawn.

I noticed the Italians expelling a few dark bees, which I assumed to be the queen's original retainers, and wondered if there was a racial problem in the hive— unheard of among bees. The snow left, but weather continued semi-rotten from the day they arrived, raw, overcast, and drizzly. But the other, established colonies were growing normally, if grumpily.

Then I made a full check on the first glorious blue-skyed and sunny day and found the problem. The new inner cover was a cheap one, Masonite in thin wood rails, and the fiberboard had warped a bit around the bee-escape cutout. The wood plank I'd carelessly tossed over the cutout hole had crushed a bee and its carcass had kept the board from sealing to the warped top. Further, where the corners of the rails joined, there were holes where the grooves had been cut out. Those four little flues combined with the unsealed cutout to draw heat up and out of the hive like a smokestack. The poor bees weren't bigots or lazy at all, but were expending all their time and energy keeping the queen and a small amount of brood warm in a drafty home. The dark bees I saw being kicked out must have been interlopers from another colony.

Feeling like an inadequate provider, I put on a proper cover and replaced the Boardman entrance feeder with an inside-the-hive division board feeder to make it easier for my little wards to fuel up.

They never did get beyond the initial four frames and swarmed the first week of July, the remaining Italians from the package and hatched Carniolans together. The ill treatment had little effect. I caught and hived the swarm, fed it with a division board feeder for a month, and it grew fast enough to produce a full super of beautiful late summer honey that year, honey that I didn't deserve one bit (though I did have to give most of it back to tide them through the following spring).

The original colony was given a replacement Buckfast queen in a four-frame nuc, produced no surplus, but put up enough stores to keep it through winter and into a fine second season.

In all, I got two thriving colonies for the coming year, and almost a super of surplus honey. Had I been more careful, I probably would have had one colony—but several times the surplus honey that first year. It's a fact that one strong colony will outproduce several weaker ones.

Examining Frames

When inspecting a frame, hold it firmly by the top. It will be covered with bees and surprisingly heavy. Gently brush off the bees if needed for a good look at the brood. New comb is eating-tender and can break if you offend its structural integrity, so keep it hanging vertically.

To examine the reverse side, put the frame down and grasp it from the other side or revolve your wrist and turn it like the page of a book. (Here's where the frame holder is a boon.) To see the cell contents easily, stand with the sun behind one shoulder and angle the bottom of the frame toward you slightly so light floods the cell interiors. The upper inch or so of the comb will probably be filled with nectar or honey made largely from your sugar syrup, possibly already capped with snow-white wax. Below that will be a thin arc of cells partly packed with varicolored pollen. And below that, most of the frame will be filled with developing young. Here is what you should see on drawn frames at this two-week inspection:

1. Eggs. From about the third day after introduction of the queen, eggs like little white commas on a printed page will be pointing up from where they are fastened at the bottom of cells. The presence of bands of eggs in a wide arc or thick circle patterns toward the center of the comb—one egg to a cell—will confirm that the queen is laying. If there is none, and you are sure the queen has been released and out for several days, order a new queen immediately. Eggs are tiny. Look closely.

2. Larvae. From the sixth day and on, there should be circular or arced bands of eggs plus small white grub-like larvae curled at cell bottoms, hatched from eggs three days after being laid, and proving that the eggs are viable. Nurse bees will be tending them, feeding the salivary excretion called royal jelly to all larvae for the first three days, then a ration including honey and pollen. The larvae should be enough larger than eggs to be obvious at a glance within ten days after the queen is introduced, which is why you should wait at least that time to open the hive. If there are eggs, but no larvae, wait a week and check again. Then, if no eggs have hatched, a new queen is needed.

3. Capped Brood. From about the twelfth day on, you should see areas of brood under cappings. In their ninth day, worker larvae go into the pupal stage, spinning a cocoon under a little lid of opaque yellow wax that is distinct from the translucent white wax covering honey. They will emerge on the twenty-first day as full adults, will groom themselves, find something to eat, and get right to work nursing the larvae. Later in your beekeeping career you will probably see the brood emerge, nibbling their individual way through the wax capping. It's a thrill to see the little feelers poking through the cappings. But let the coincidence happen. Don't keep opening the hive and disturbing the bees just to witness a bee birth.

If all looks well according to the above timetable, plus or minus a few days, and the bees are grumpy, you can close the hive. Otherwise, before you replace the frames and close up, admire the queen's handiwork more closely and see if you can pick her out on the comb. Queen spotting is an important beekeeping skill, necessary when you replace a defective or elderly queen. That's called re-queening. We will discuss it in detail later.

Finding the Queen

In rare instances, the queen may be cruising the nest and be on hive walls or frame tops or inner cover, momentarily resting from her labors. If I spot her wandering, I close the hive. Queens that aren't actively laying can be confused by the sudden light, and may remember their courting days, forget the family, and take wing to be lost forever. The colony will have new larvae to build a queen cell around and feed up into a new queen, but you will lose a crucial two weeks and more, the new queen will breed with local drones, and you'll have no idea of paternal genetics, thus the characteristics they'll impart to your bees.

Odds are, the queen will be on comb containing new eggs and intent on laying more. Hold the comb at easy forearm's length over the hive and watch the moving pattern of bee activity.

I find I can discern patterns in the sea of bees by looking out of the corner of my eye or gazing with eyes unfocused.

Look for a Circle

Every bee will be moving independently but for the crew around the queen. All the bees in the circle immediately surrounding the queen will face her, and this little spoked-wheel shape will

QUEEN
AND ATTENDANTS

move on the comb as she wanders along sticking her head into cell after cell, then inserting her abdomen to lay an egg in those that pass muster. Finding this moving doughnut of bees is the best way to spot the queen; it is an island of comparative consistency in a sea of randomly moving bees. There will be groups of bees digging around in cells, and gangs of them apparently interested in the same segment of comb, but no group will have the spoked-wheel configuration unless the queen is inside. Once seen, the queen will stand out as considerably longer in the abdomen, usually with less distinct striping, and often a bit lighter in color than the others. Be patient in your search; like everything in beekeeping, the indicators are subtle and take time to learn. Professional queen spotters can find queens in seconds. It takes me several trips sometimes.

The Brood

The queen forms her brood in an ellipsoid, football shape on several adjacent frames. Bees just naturally form rounded solids when they coalesce, witness the hanging cluster in the shipping cage or a swarm. Center frames will be filled with brood cells except at the top and corners, while only the center of the next-to-outer frames will contain brood. The queen goes from frame to frame, laying eggs in almost every cell in circular or arc-shaped patterns across the comb. You will find sections of similar-aged larvae alternating with new eggs, and later in the season with capped and emerging brood and sectors of empty cells cleaned and awaiting the queen's next visit.

If the queen is a good one, most of the cells in a segment will contain brood. All of them never do, as even the best queens will miss a cell now and again, and workers will remove the inevitable defective eggs and larvae.

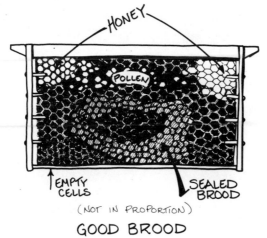

HONEY

POLLEN

EMPTY CELLS

SEALED BROOD

(NOT IN PROPORTION)

GOOD BROOD

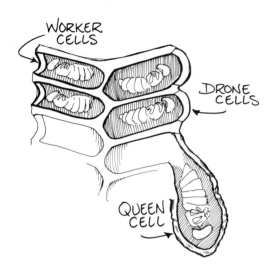

WORKER CELLS

DRONE CELLS

QUEEN CELL

Drones

It's more common among older queens, but a few new queens will be drone-layers, unable to fertilize their eggs – and only an egg that has been united with stored sperm will produce a worker bee. Unfertilized but viable eggs produce males, the bumbling drones that are worthless to your working colony. To check for this rare problem, wait until the brood is capped. Cappings of worker cells will be just slightly raised above cell top level. Each has a little pit in the center. Drone cappings are distinctly domed, even when topping worker-sized cells characteristic of a drone-laying queen. Workers may let excessive drone brood die. It will smell rotten and may give you a disease scare, but it will have drone caps and won't have the disease characteristics described in Chapter 9.

In time, you'll find larger-than-normal cells with rounded cappings containing normally developing drones. These will be at the margins of the brood, with a few scattered among worker cells, often squeezing several smaller cells aside. There are always a few, and the drone population builds to several hundred in swarming season. If many cells in the central worker brood areas have those domed drone caps, you should replace the queen.

If a great many cells among the brood appear empty and there is no sign of disease, your queen may be producing **diploid drones**, with a matching set of **sex alleles** in their twin-chromosome genetic makeup. **Unmatched** allele pairs produce normal workers, while unfertilized eggs having only a **single** allele from the queen produce drones. The **matched** alleles produce a bee with incompatible sex genes, and they don't develop. Up to half the eggs laid can be so affected. Workers remove the non-viable eggs, but the young queen won't normally visit the cell again until viable brood has emerged.

Either problem of excess drone production is irremediable, the latter a result of inbreeding, and you should call the supplier for an immediate replacement queen unless you're so disappointed you decide to replace suppliers (which I would do).

THE SPRING PROGRESSES

To stimulate comb construction and fuel brood rearing, while waiting for brood to hatch and package house bees to graduate to forager status, keep feeding sugar syrup for at least a month after a good queen is confirmed to be laying, or until all comb is drawn and there is heavy forager flight activity at the hive entrance. At least one forager arriving per second is my rule of thumb.

While the population builds, watch for congestion around the entrance reducer/feeder. When bees cluster at the entrance waiting to get in, it's time to give them more in-and-out space. Replace the entrance reducer with one having a larger entry. Or remove the reducer altogether, insert the feeder's thicker inner lip under the hive body proper, and install small wood blocks, strips of window screen, or small stones—anything to keep the entrance just large enough to permit bees to leave and enter without congestion, but not so large as to overtax guard bees. You will want to vary the opening as the population grows in spring, then diminishes in fall, or abruptly halves after a swarm.

I've sawed lumber into ¾″ square strips varying in length from 3″ blocks to hive-width entrance cleats of 14″ to 15″. The full-width cleats have conventional ⅜″ high openings of verying lengths. I put in what seems to be needed.

Objectives

This first spring and in the many more to come, you'll be working with three interrelated objectives:

1. **To obtain from your bees the maximum return in satisfaction, which depends on your ability to**

2. **Thwart the colonies' natural swarming urge and direct their brood-building efforts to increase and retain colony strength, which will in turn give you**

3. **An optimum harvest of honey and wax, which is the major tangible benefit of keeping bees and determinant of beekeeping satisfaction (but not the only one—as we'll see).**

First Year Harvest

The expert books tell you not to expect surplus honey your first year with package bees. Don't believe them. With top stock and equipment, generous feeding, a little luck, and good swarm management, you can do it. I did my first year, despite swarms. First, though, you must learn to recognize, anticipate, and manage the swarming cycle. By the sixth to eighth week, a new colony's numbers may begin to exceed carrying capacity of the brood chamber. It is then, when population is high and the major summer honey-flows are still in the offing, that the bees' normal reproductive instinct boils up, even from a newly hived swarm or package.

Bees will build swarm cells, which contain growing queens. When they are about to emerge, the old queen and up to 90 percent of the colony fly off to a new nest, leaving frames of emerging brood to start a new colony for the young queen. When the countdown to the swarm is under way, workers suspend foraging and the old queen stops laying and begins to slim down preparatory to flight. By then, there is precious little a mere human can do to stop them beyond breaking up the colony.

There are dozens of fancy swarm-prevention techniques you can try, but as Dr. C.C. Miller says in *Fifty Years Among the Bees*: "If a colony disposed to swarm should be blown up with dynamite, it would probably not . . . swarm. . . ." But otherwise it will. Nobody can stop a swarm, and no one is 100 percent successful, or even 50 percent successful, some years in preventing swarms.

Among probable causes that you can eliminate to avoid swarming are:

- Crowding in the hive, thus insufficient space for the queen to lay eggs and for brood to be raised, and workers to store and ripen incoming nectar.

- Poor hive ventilation combined with high heat, humidity, and a wet hive base.

- Changeable weather and temperature, creating an erratic nectar and pollen flow insufficient to the colony's brood-rearing needs. These are conditions that only the bees can identify with certainty, and that we can only hope to ameliorate with care and feeding.

- The queen's characteristics, particularly her age, which can reduce production of the pheromone that inhibits construction of queen cells.

Proper Ventilation

As the colony grows, moisture released by bee respiration and by evaporation of nectar will increase to the point that ventilating bees may not be able to remove it through the hive entrance. Drops will condense on the inner cover and run down frames and hive sides to puddle on the baseboard, encouraging rot in the wood and disease in the bees.

As soon as weather becomes consistently warm enough that I can be sure the bees are able to maintain comb temperatures without help (day temperatures well above the bees' 57° flying minimum), I remove the board covering the cutout in the inner cover to increase ventilation. In another few weeks, especially if I find water on the baseboard or inner cover, I will cut a half-inch wide notch in the lower front rim of the cover and pull the telescoping cover forward to let more moisture escape with rising heat from the hive. Air flow can be regulated by moving the telescoping cover back and forth.

Wet Bottom Boards

Excess moisture on the bottom board makes temperature control difficult, but is a problem that can be readily cured. You've done most of the job by placing your hives at a slight incline on a foundation that's well off the ground. If the bottom board wood appears to be getting soggy, mildewing in the cracks perhaps, get the hive into the sun. Move it a foot at a time so the forager bees won't lose their bearing and drift, to join the work force of other hives.

Signs of Crowding

A sure sign of ventilation problems, crowding, or both is bees hanging out in clusters on the front of the hive. If this persists into the evening, it is particularly serious. On steamy days, heat and humidity inside the hive may be too high to permit the entire population to perch inside. If a good honeyflow is on, you can raise the front of the bottom hive body above the baseboard with cleats and give the bees more ventilating room. (If there is no honeyflow, this would encourage robbing.)

I staple a piece of screen over the cutout in the inner cover, and can push the telescoping cover back to uncover the opening during hot days. In particularly warm climates, many beekeepers fashion a screen cover and install it in place of an inner cover. By removing or blocking up the telescoping cover, they permit full-hive ventilation in extreme heat or when they are transporting a full colony being kept in the hive as it is moved to another location during a hot day.

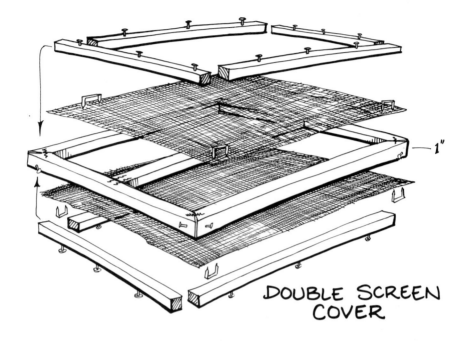

DOUBLE SCREEN
COVER

Swarm Checks

After your package bees have been working for four weeks, and in succeeding years, once the early spring pollen and nectar season has begun and the spring population buildup is well under way, make quick two-phase swarm-prevention inspections at least once a week, though twice a week is better in peak swarming season. A colony commits to swarm when the queen larvae are capped, only seven days after the eggs are laid. The workers will begin to act logy, foraging will diminish, and many bees will loaf around waiting for the swarm. In nine more days, the young queens begin to stir in their drooping cells. Before they emerge, the swarm is gone.

Back in the nest, the first queen to emerge may go around stinging her rivals in their cells. Or, the virgin queens may lead one or several after-swarms, leaving the nest empty but for a single young queen, a skeleton force of nurse bees, and the developing brood. Such a colony will do well to put up its own winter stores, say nothing of surplus honey. You must do all possible to prevent the swarm from developing.

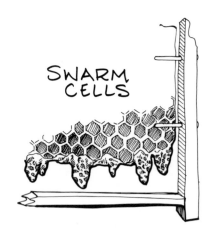

SUPERSEDURE CELLS

SWARM CELLS

The first part of the swarm check for crowding requires a quick peek under the inner cover in the warmth of late afternoon after foragers are home. If crowded, bees will be packed into a circle on the inner cover over all frames that are filled with working or roosting bees. Colonies often swarm before the outer frames are fully covered. So when the cover over the six to eight inner frames is packed with bees, add a second brood chamber or put on a super, depending on your harvest objectives and queen/brood management plan. If you add another box too soon, the bees will chew up the foundation. Add it too late and they will swarm for sure.

Add a Hive Body

If the inner cover looks crowded, plan to add a second brood chamber or a super immediately, but first go to phase two of the quick swarm check. Use your hive tool to crack the hive body from the bottom board. Slide it forward several inches so the center of gravity rests at mid-base, and tilt it high enough to see the bottoms of the frames clearly. If need be, smoke the bees. If swarming preparations are in progress, a half dozen or more variously shaped and sized swarm cells for hatching queens will be protruding from the bottoms of the comb. They hang down and are dimpled and about an inch long, looking much like peanut shells. Empty cell starts, looking like acorn caps, are nothing to worry about; leave them, but continue to check twice weekly for further development. If swarm cells contain larvae or are capped, a swarm is building and you should take action.

If queen cells containing larvae aren't capped, the swarm can probably be avoided by removing the cells and two to four frames of sealed brood with adhering bees. Replace the brood frames with frames containing new foundation. Add this brood to weak colonies, which will accept young bees without a quibble. Or make up a nuc; either give it a new queen or include one frame containing queen cells. With no old queen to lead, the nuc shouldn't swarm. Sell the nuc or let it expand into a new colony.

If Cells Are Capped

If the swarm cells are capped, a swarm is almost certain. You can try one of the elaborate manipulations recorded in the literature or resign yourself to a swarm and try to manage it.

Here is the only system that works for me—some of the time. It's a version of the padgening process, named (but with the spelling changed) like most bee manipulations after its inventor or first popularizer, a nineteenth century beeman named J. W. Pagden.

I pry a few swarm cells from the bottom of the comb and put them in a little glass-topped queen-rearing nuc with an internal feeder and half-frames of brood with bees to cover. You can tell how near the queens are to emerging by opening one cell. They are about a day away when the young bee begins to show color. Swarms will usually leave as new queens emerge.

An empty hive is set up and ready to go, and I try to make sure someone is keeping an eye on the swarm-bound colony. With luck, I'll capture the swarm and install it in the empty hive at the parent colony's location, putting it back where it came from, but in a new box. The parent colony is moved several yards away; its field bees will fly back to the original location and join the swarm. I either let the original colony, now diminished by the swarm, develop independently, divide the brood and house bees among weak colonies, or dequeen and reunite in a few days with the padgened colony.

This last method lets the swarm instinct run its course and at the price of a little vigilance and a simple manipulation I have a newly revitalized, full-strength bee colony housed in new quarters and raring to begin drawing comb. It's very satisfying when you have the time and energy to make it work. Of course, the bees may swarm all over again—but such are the joys of keeping bees.

In sum, it is probably easier to accept swarm preparations if the queen cells are capped, and prepare to capture the swarm. To interrupt a swarm cycle already under way you must break down the hive, search out all swarm cells, and remove them from the comb bottoms. But there is one important caution:

If you find a few same-sized (often small) queen cells in mid-frame locations only, and none on the frame bottoms, the colony is superseding a dead or failing queen. This colony may swarm too. But never remove the supersedure cells unless you have a new queen to give the bees. We'll discuss supersedure later. For now, follow the queen cell guide.

Queen Cell Guide

Five to eight cells of uniform size and shape in mid-comb location are supersedure cells and should be left alone.

Six to twenty-plus different sized and shaped cells on the bottom of the combs and draping down over the bottom bars are swarm cells and may be removed.

Summer's Coming

As spring melds into summer, the swarming season passes, and your colonies will begin crowding their brood chamber. It is time to give them more space to grow and to store the coming harvest of liquid gold.

Chapter 6

THE GOLDEN
HARVEST

While spring matures, continue feeding your bees, even though the fruit blossoms are popping all around. The colony's prime job is to build bee strength and draw comb, and only a constant supply of food will keep them at it. The foraging population is still too small to bring in all the nectar the bees can use.

When swarm checks show a bee-covered inner cover, and a quick look indicates that seven or eight frames of foundation are well drawn and filling with brood, add the second full-depth brood chamber with ten frames, and keep on feeding. Bees draw comb best during a honeyflow, and the constant supply of sugar water mimics a round-the-clock nectar deluge to the bees. If weather is warm enough, they'll work day and night drawing comb in the second hive body.

Change Feeders

As temperatures warm and the colony builds strength, the outside feeder will become less suitable. The syrup may spoil or attract robber bees. When bee traffic has increased enough so that foragers are crowding the entry, it is time to enlarge the entrance, and you may as well remove the Boardman feeder. Turn the entrance reducer so the small opening is operational, and install a division board feeder in place of an outside frame in the upper story. Plan to leave it until most foundation in both boxes is drawn. Filling the feeder is easy. Just remove the outer cover, slide the inner cover over an inch or two, and pour in the syrup—slowly, so the bees can climb out of the way.

Planning for the Harvest

As late spring honeyflows approach, it is time to plan for the coming harvest, to select your production scheme, then ready the supers and frames that your bees will pack with liquid gold.

First, though, ask yourself what you truly want from keeping bees. Almost everything you read assumes that beekeepers seek maximum gain and that even the backyard fancier is out for a record honey yield. Top honey production and maximum income from pollinating fees are eminently reasonable goals for a commercial beekeeper, business being business whether you're keeping a store, a medical practice, or bees.

But that's work, and most of us do enough of that as it is. Beekeeping on a backyard scale is labor, to be sure, and a more productive way to spend Sunday afternoon than sitting in front of the TV. But let's not restrict the rewards of beekeeping to pounds of honey or dollars and cents made or saved.

I'm content with enough honey to meet the needs of family and friends and to enjoy the indirect fruits of the bees' pollinating efforts, the apples and cucumbers and strawberries we harvest each year.

Not to get sentimental, but I find plenty of intangible rewards in working bees. Learning their ways is pure fascination. Bees are better natural science instructors than any I had in school. It's a quiet pleasure to watch them buzz happily, if unpaid, as they pollinate the dandelions and goldenrod. When all covered with golden pollen, they are positively attractive creatures. As our son, Sam, observed some years ago: "They're cute and fuzzy, aren't they, Daddy? Like little teddy bears."

There's an almost paternal satisfaction in offering a super to the colony, fretting through the days the bees ignore it utterly, then watching them eagerly move in to begin drawing comb and packing in the nectar and honey.

Pulling a super, especially your first one, loaded with beautiful honeycomb is an undeniable thrill. And that fresh, unprocessed honey does have a tang and heady aroma you'll never find in the bottled product. But it's just a part of the satisfaction of keeping bees.

Try to decide your top priority. Are you keeping bees primarily to harvest the honey, or is the honey a justification (if you need one) for keeping the bees? If you pick the former, I look forward to reading of your 500-pound record in a coming issue of the bee magazines. If you pick the latter, that's two of us.

The Supering Scheme

In choosing a plan for harvesting honey, you should weigh the trade-offs in time, equipment, and attention needed against your desired return in wax, honey, and satisfaction.

Here are some choices:

1. If you're primarily attracted by the quiet pleasure of working with the little creatures on weekends, you may be content with a couple of easygoing colonies and a super or two of comb honey each year to justify your time to family and friends.

2. Do you demand top output from yourself, the maximum tangible return for your time and effort? You will probably want to expand quickly to a dozen multiple brood-chamber/multiple-super hives and more. That could mean 300 pounds of extracted honey and up a year and you may want to set up an extracting room, particularly if you enjoy owning and operating precision machinery. That may get you into large-scale *out-apiaries*, assemblages of colonies in locations near the nectar, and eventually into honey production or a pollinating service. Godspeed!

3. Got a natural scientist's curiosity? Perhaps you'll find five or six colonies perfect for trying complicated brood manipulations, dual-queen schemes, and complex swarm-control plans. Perhaps you'll try queen-raising, artificial insemination, or hybridizing, or work to discover a new bee behavior or perfect a new management system. Come up with something really novel, write an article for *Gleanings*. . . or *American Bee Journal*, and name the discovery for yourself. Become an expert, teach the Scouts or conduct beekeeping courses at the local college, or take on a line of beeware for local sale.

4. On the other hand, you may derive pleasure from creating small, perfect things, preferring a few jewel-like frames of section honey to gallons of liquid. You might be happiest trying beeway section supers or Ross Rounds in a few carefully monitored and intensively managed and manipulated colonies.

See the Supering Shopping List for a guide to purchasing your honey-harvesting equipment. Any method is good beekeeping. I know of few other spare-time activities that can satisfy as wide a range of human needs. Just be sure you are harvesting your way, for your reasons. Become your own expert on your own apiary, and relegate the published experts to a proper place on the bookshelf—present company included.

Ways to Produce Honey

Here are your honey production options, with major advantages and disadvantages of each. I must acknowledge that not all beekeepers will agree with me. From this point on, beekeeping becomes as much of an individual art as a science or craft. Your ideas and experience are as valid as mine or anyone else's. With a solid dual-chamber hive housing each colony, you are ready to enlarge, combine, or split colonies in order to adopt any of the options.

1. Extracting honey offers the most output per colony from the most straightforward management scheme. Drawn, filled, and capped honeycomb is removed and the cappings are cut off. The honey is removed with a mechanical extractor and the comb is reintroduced into the hive. In an area of good bee forage in a good year you can just keep stacking the supers on and taking them off; ten supers to a hive is not unheard of, and four or five is relatively common. In a poor year you can extract when no other system will produce. However, the bees need time and nectar to draw comb, so unless you can use full plastic frames, you won't get to full production for a year or more.

You need to buy or borrow uncapping knives, an extractor, and bottling equipment, and either buy new containers or save, wash, and sterilize recycled glass food jars. Wax output is restricted to cappings, and wax moth-proof storage for frames with empty comb is essential.

It is difficult to sell home-produced extracted honey to stores for a reasonable price due to low-price competition from large-scale domestic producers who have a hard time of their own with lower priced (and in some cases, government-subsidized) competition from abroad. The liquid gold is a commodity like sugar or molasses in many shoppers' minds and not easy to sell direct.

2. Comb honey, which is used wax and all, offers less overall output than extracted—considerably less when you realize that it takes eight pounds of honey to produce a single pound of wax. But you get honeycomb for use as is or for crushing into liquid honey and wax for candles. It takes a little more beekeeper time and skill than extracting, and you lose some cash since the foundation must be replaced each time the honey is harvested. Unless, that is, you might enjoy the challenge of making a foundation press and producing your own eating foundation from your own wax as I do; details are explained elsewhere. In any event, there is no investment in extracting or bottling equipment and you don't need space to store empty comb.

The final comb honey product sells well in specialty stores and roadside stands. It can be packaged in three ways:

A. In the frame, sold as it comes from the hive (only fully packed frames with clean white cappings).

B. As cut comb; sections of comb cut and drained and sold in clear plastic boxes.

C. Chunk honey; pieces of comb (usually from frames the bees haven't completely filled with perfect honey cells) in a jar, and the container filled with liquid honey.

3. Producing comb honey in sections is doing it the old-fashioned way. Bees are forced to build honeycomb in small square wooden or round plastic forms. This can be productive in the hands of a dedicated beekeeper, but requires the most involved management plans, much experience, and, some feel, intuitive skill. You need special supers and must purchase the little frames that hold the honey. This sells best of any in specialty outlets and from roadside stands if packaged attractively.

We'll cover all three approaches, but I must admit a bias in favor of the backyard beekeeper's special, reasonable quantities of comb honey.

A SUPERING SHOPPING LIST

For each colony that will be strong enough to produce surplus honey in a given year you should have:

- **2 supers (at minimum): full, ¾, or half-depth (the last are lightest and easiet to manipulate)**
- **20 frames**
- **20 sheets of foundation**

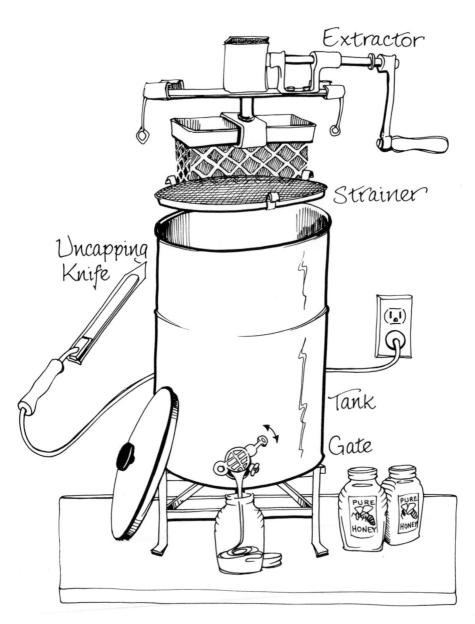

Extractor

Strainer

Uncapping
Knife

Tank

Gate

PURE
HONEY

PURE
HONEY

EXTRACTING GEAR

- 80 support pins
- 1 queen excluder
- 1 bee escape (Porter escape or an escape board such as ARTB's maze design)

For Extracting

If extracting, your frames should be top quality and your foundation reinforced to hold up to the extractor. You will also need to buy or find access to:

- A decapping knife (an electric model is vastly easier)
- A stainless steel tank with a screen top to drain cappings
- A centrifugal extractor

Not essential, but helpful is a stainless steel tank with a strainer and honey gate to clarify and bottle the honey. A heated model makes things go faster – but that's getting into considerable expense for a backyard beekeeper.

For Comb Honey

To produce comb honey in any form, all you need besides the supers are extra frames and foundation. The foundation should be the thinnest (and least expensive) available. I don't even put support pins in my homemade foundation for comb honey.

Too Much of A Good Thing

Before you decide on a production scheme and begin assembling supers, bear in mind that a full shallow super contains twenty to thirty pounds of honey. How much does your family use in a year? Honest, now. A single jar lasts forever in some homes. You need a satisfying appreciative outlet for your honey to reward you for the time and effort that goes into it. I've seen some new beekeepers overwhelmed with it, having too little for processing and sale to USDA-grade standards and too much to use or give away. It's kind of like all those beautiful tomatoes that you (and I, and most gardeners) have in super abundance in August. Tomatoes can be fed to the chickens, sneaked into the compost, or ignored. But honey? It is wonderful in baking, but not everyone has time to bake, and granulated sugar is tasteless but for the sweetness, and easier to measure and clean up after. The kids quickly tire of honey as an everyday topping on pancakes and peanut butter sandwiches. It is grand in herbal teas but ruins the taste of conventional tea or coffee. So, what do you do with any excess? Some U.S. hobby beekeepers have put their surplus honey under a federal CCC loan, but that program is following other government subsidies into oblivion in the era of deregulation. You can't throw it out. How could you face all those loyal little bees working their lives away to store honey that you robbed from them, and now you can't find a proper use for it?

The burden of disposing of too much honey can drive an over-enthusiastic beekeeper out of beekeeping. So, think carefully before you make a heavy financial investment in multiple colonies or extracting gear, or an emotional investment in expectation of only the maximum tangible reward from beekeeping.

The Honeyflow

The bees' preferred source of nectar is not always apparent to human senses. They harvest whichever plant offers the greatest return for their time and effort. Every spring our bees bypass a luridly fragrant honeysuckle bush located smack in front of one dual hive stand, a bush humming with native solitary bees, nectar flies, and bumblebees, in favor of some mysterious flower I can never identify. But you can be (almost) sure the bees will harvest the major late spring/early summer nectar sources in your locale. Local beekeepers are your best guides to honeyflow amounts and timing, but see Nectar Sources in Chapter 2 for some guidelines.

Years when the fifty acres of clover across the road erupt with bloom practically overnight, I know our field bees will be working it from the third day from blossoming until the flower heads begin to brown, as house bees slave night and day to make room and evaporate the incoming nectar. At the end of this flow, I pull any partly filled supers and reload them with frames and new foundation. It's nice to brag about pure single-source honey when you can, but it's seldom possible in our locale, where most flows are mixtures of wild flower nectar. I have had pure dandelion honey in spring and goldenrod honey in the fall, both with a bitter aftertaste. We tried pure buckwheat honey some years back when we grew buckwheat as a green manure. The honey was almost purple and so strong tasting we left most of it for the bees.

Someday I am going to pack a few colonies in the truck and spend a season as a migratory beekeeper, amassing a collection of pure supers of tupelo and orange blossom and basswood and fireweed and all the really prime honeys from around the continent. Could be an interesting book: *Travels With Apis m.* Want to make up a caravan?

The Honeyflow Test

If the bloom can be in the treetops, distant fields, or scattered all over, how can you tell whether a flow is on or not? If the weather has been consistently warm and sunny, your bees sound contented, and the foragers are flying eagerly, the bloom probably is a good one. But if weather has been overcast and cool for several days, flowering may be delayed or nectar supply severely diminished. Or conditions may appear good, but the plants just aren't blooming. This is frequently the case in summer and fall. If the colony is at or near full strength, they may need to dive into stores to stay alive and keep the brood coming on. This runs counter to their hoarding instinct, and just a few days of it during a peak population season can trigger a swarm.

To double-check for presence of a nectar flow in good weather, when bees act grumpy, I fill a jar lid with honey and put it on a white paper plate in the sun on the old stone barn foundation midway between the three backyard double-hive stands. The occasional bee will always come by to check it out and native bees and wasps may find it irresistible. But if a large number of honeybees is feeding within a couple of hours, I'm sure the nectar spigot is off for the time being. I feed sparingly until honeyflow restarts.

When to Super

Add a super when the bees are ready for it. This may sound too obvious to warrant mention, but if you put on foundation too early, the bees will gnaw the wax out and use it elsewhere in the nest. Better to add supers too early, though, than to wait too long and have your bees swarm.

One test of readiness is bee count. Tick off incoming honey foragers. If they number two per second over a minute or so, you may be ready. Check the inner cover some evening when field bees are back. If all of the inner cover but the corners is crowded with bees, a super is almost certainly needed. To be fully sure, get a super ready, but before putting it on, look down into the hive; if bees are working all frame faces except perhaps the outer sides of the end frames, it's time for that new super. If you see them applying a fresh layer of white wax to the top of combs, or "white waxing," as the old-timers say, the super is overdue. In other words, put on a super just before the bees get so crowded that they begin to think about swarming.

Bees will move most eagerly into ready drawn, preused extracting comb. A strong colony can fill and cap a complete super of drawn comb in a day or two, though I've never seen it. If you lack drawn comb, your first super must contain frames with foundation — deep or shallow size, wired for a second brood chamber or for extracting, or thin foundation for fully edible comb honey, as you wish. Don't try section supers first. The bees won't go to work in the sections without a strong honeyflow and may need some kind of bait such as drawn comb or a drawn and partly filled super above.

I tried a super of lovely basswood Beeway sections my first bee year. The bees refused to move up and the colony swarmed all spring and summer. I tried putting honey on the frames. This did no good. Then I tried sprinkling sugar on the inner cover over the section super. They ignored this too. I even tried smoking the bees. They fled the smoke, but returned to the brood chamber as soon as the smoker went cold.

Save section supers until you have conventional frames all or partly filled to act as bait for the bees.

Queen Excluders

The queen excluder permits workers to pass, but holds back a laying queen, so keeps brood out of honeycomb. It goes between supers and the brood chamber. Don't use them if you don't need to, because they retard worker travel.

Don't put a queen excluder between brood nest and a first super at the outset, or the bees may resist moving up to draw comb. You may not need an excluder at all if frame tops in the brood nest are well-filled with honey and you are using shallow supers. Queens don't like to cross honey (which in the wild goes at the top of the nest), and they consider shallow supers too short for a proper laying pattern.

Attracting the Bees

If the bees don't move onto the foundation, you may try several tricks. You can bait the super with three or four frames of drawn but empty comb, obtained your first year from a fellow beekeeper who doesn't have brood disease in his apiary. (A recent bee inspection certificate is the most reliable indicator.)

With two brood chambers, put a super of foundation between them, with queen excluders at top and bottom, so you don't have to worry which hive body the queen is using. Or put the super under the brood chamber so foragers have to traverse it to talk with the house bees, who should get the idea and begin to draw comb to store incoming nectar. You don't need an excluder for this, as the queen instinctively moves up in the hive.

Warning: any excluder placed between brood nest and bottom for any length of time will trap the drones inside along with the queen. They won't be able to get out and do their job, will panhandle for food full time, and may become such a nuisance the workers refuse to let them eat. They'll die, clog the extruder, and . . . well, don't let it happen. Use such an arrangement just long enough to get the workers moved into the super.

Another trick is to move several frames of advanced or capped brood into a super of foundation, replacing them in the brood nest with frames of foundation, and hope bees following the brood will draw the foundation and begin storing honey. Be sure the queen is not on the brood, and put on an excluder immediately or the queen may want to follow the kids, especially into a top super. Once comb is being drawn, put the frames of brood back where they were.

Tricks or no, if there is not a strong honeyflow, no bee unmotivated by swarm instinct will go into a super and draw out comb. The only trick I use is to feed them.

Peek under the covers every day or so to see when the bees move into the super. There will always be a few young bees wandering around and loafing there, and you may begin to fret, but don't. Just feed the bees if you suspect no honeyflow and keep up the swarm checks. Then one day the workers will sweep in and get to work. What a kick that is! You'll have immediate visions of all the relatives opening up jars or combs of beautiful, golden honey over the next holiday season.

When eight of the frames are drawn and a quick check shows frames about half-full of honey or nectar and capped honey at the tops of some combs, add another super atop the first. Make sure the queen is with the brood, then you can add a queen excluder over the brood nest, as bees will be drawn through to work the initial super. Some beekeepers advise waiting until the first super is almost full before adding a second, but I feel it's better to add more supering space than needed during the early honeyflow when swarming is a danger, then add less later in the season to encourage bees to finish up the frames they have.

Supering Sequence

If you want maximum output and are willing to invest in the equipment, you can adopt the conventional three-to-five super plan. Add them in the order illustrated. Put on a new super when the one just before it is about half-full and the one preceding that

SUPERING SEQUENCE:

is largely full. Put each new super of foundation at the top of the stack. Under it go earlier supers in descending order of age.

For some reason, bees fill out comb at the rear of the hive before the front, so rotate supers front-to-back with each shift in location. This system takes a lot of lifting, but seems to encourage the bees to finish off supers. This is more important in comb honey than extracted.

If you will extract immediately or have freezer space for comb honey, take off supers when all frames are filled and capped. This will reduce lifting and the number of little bee footprints that in time will discolor the capping wax. Or, leave them on and the bees will control wax moth larvae for you. Don't extract uncapped, thus uncured, honey. It will spoil.

To remove bees from frames to be harvested, you can brush them off with the bee brush. Then take the frames with the few bees that are sure to be hanging on into the kitchen or wherever you'll process honey. Turn off all the lights, pull the window shades, and open the kitchen door. The bees will fly out and back to their hive. If flies come in, close the screen door; bees will group there and you can release them at will.

A gas-engine-powered hi-volume/lo-pressure commercial bee blower is fun, but costs $100 and more. You can use a shop vac with the hose in the exhaust outlet and a narrow nozzle on the tip. Bees don't mind being blown off frames so long as the force doesn't slam them against something.

A commercial fume board uses a noxious gas to drive bees down off supers, but that stinks—literally.

Most backyard beekeepers install a Porter bee escape in the cut-out in the inner cover, and put the cover under the top super. Bees can get out of that super but not back in unless weather is so hot and bee travel both ways so fast they crowd the escape springs, in which case the excluder doesn't exclude very well. Ordinarily, though, the super will be clear in twenty-four hours. The bee escape seems to work best in a screen board. Some beekeepers favor boards with multiple escapes.

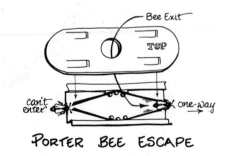

PORTER BEE ESCAPE

WHY THEY HANG AROUND

You've placed the bee escape in the inner cover, placed the cover beneath the super to be cleared of bees, placed the outer cover on top of the super.

After waiting two days for the bees to clear out, you look in and, to your surprise and disappointment, you find business as usual.

Here are three possible reasons why the bees are still there.

1. Bees, and perhaps they are the larger drones, are caught in the small springs of the escape, halting all traffic through it. Check the escape and clear it.

2. You've left a route open so the bees can return. Is there a ventilation hole drilled in the super? The inner cover has a ventilation port cut in the rim. Are the bees returning through that port? Close up tight.

3. The bees want to stay. If the queen had a chance to lay eggs in the super, the bees won't desert them, but will wait until the bees have emerged and are ready to leave the hive. The only remedy is more time. Or, if you are in a hurry, smoke the bees down. Then brush them off, frame by frame.

TECHNIQUES FOR EXTRACTING HONEY

If you want to extract exclusively, I'd suggest trying at least one super of the full-comb plastic frames. My own limited experiments have been disappointing, but being a comb honey fan, I've not pursued it. Reportedly, the newer designs with deep cells, sold prewaxed, are acceptable to bees in many localities. The plastic is costly ($5 and up a frame), but lasts forever and is worth a try by new extractors.

If you are using conventional frames, you must get bees to draw supers on reinforced foundation—the plastic-backed such as Dadant's Duragilt, Root's 3-Ply, or crimp-wired foundation that is also supported with support pins or (better) with horizontal wires. The horizontals are inserted using a wiring frame, a heated spur wheel, and some practice. But extracting is hard on comb and the time is well spent. Frame wiring equipment is sold by most large suppliers.

You can't extract honey without proper equipment; honey is too viscous to flow out of the tiny cells without a lot of persuasion. I strongly advise beginners to find an established beekeeper and borrow or rent the gear for a first extraction. An extracting party, where several beekeepers share the work and one another's company, is a great way to spend a weekend afternoon.

Kitchen Scale Extracting

The first step in extracting is to cut the cappings from the honeycomb on each side of each frame. Arrange a large pan under the frame to catch the honey, and have a colander, lined with damp cheesecloth, to catch the cappings as you cut them off.

Ideally, you will have an electric or steam-heated uncapping knife to remove that top layer of each frame. Practically, the backyard beekeeper may not, but will use the two largest knives in the house, with blades a bit longer than the distance from the top to the bottom of the frame. You'll need a pan of hot water, so you can alternate knives, always working with a hot one, since wax cuts much easier with a hot blade.

Experiment to find the handiest way of holding a frame so that it's perpendicular to the edge of the colander, even slightly tilted over it, so cappings peel away from the frame. Cut the cappings from the bottom up, using the top and bottom of the frame as guides, and letting the cappings drop into the colander. As you finish a frame, place it in the extractor.

When you have finished all of the frames, make a bag of the cheesecloth in the colander, hang it over the pan in a warm room, and let it drain overnight. Most of the honey will drain out of the cuttings in that time.

Spinning the Frames

When spinning the honey out of the frames, to avoid putting too much strain on the honeycomb, turn slowly at first. Crank at less than top speed, or about 200 revolutions per minute, for two or three minutes. This will remove about half the honey from one side of the frames. Then reverse the frames and spin again at the same speed for two or three minutes. Now increase the speed to 375 revolutions per minute for several minutes, reverse the frames again and spin at the faster speed.

Honey spins out of the individual cells far easier and more quickly if the frames are warm from the hive, have been stored in a warm room, or are heated in a very cool oven, less than 100° F.

Bees Will Clean Cells

To get the supers completely cleared of honey, place them back in the hives. If there is a continuing honeyflow, the bees will refill them. If not, they will move every drop remaining to the supers they're filling. Bees will complete this chore for you in two or three days.

It's important that the frames get this final polish before they are stored. Otherwise, honey remaining in the cells will crystallize, and tend to speed crystallization of honey supplies put in them in the future.

Straining and Storing

Extracted honey should be crystal clear. You must strain it through a commercial strainer or cheesecloth. It will pour very slowly from the extractor's honey gate (that slices through the thick stream to cut off the flow—a neat trick). With time and patience, the backyard beekeeper can strain room-temperature honey. It goes faster, though if you warm the honey by leaving the tank (well sealed against bees) in full sun over an afternoon or heat it with an electric immersion coil or in a commercial hot tank. Don't heat the honey any hotter than 100° F. (just warm enough to feel) or the flavor can be ruined. Then, cool it as quickly as possible.

Package your lovely, clear honey in clear, wide-mouthed glass jars. A separate tank with a honey gate is a great help in filling jars. Seal with close-fitting lids and design a label with the name of your apiary, the date of harvest, and nectar source of your honey.

Keeping from getting sticky is a high priority in honey processing, and with practice you can work at it all day and never touch a drop—until clean-up time. Then, everything involved must be scrubbed clean or you will attract ants and other honey-loving pests.

Comb Honey Techniques

Comb honey is harvested and eaten wax and all, a delightful and old-fashioned way to enjoy the sweet stuff. Bees won't draw comb unless they feel the need for more brood space, roosting room, or a place to put more nectar. You've provided them with ample brood space in your double brood chambers, so unless they are crowded or are enjoying a strong honeyflow, they won't draw comb.

If you are content with one or possibly two supers per hive in a good year, you can let your double-chamber colonies draw and fill what supers they will. Add supers the conventional way, and just harvest them, wax and all. Stop the harvest in late summer and let the bees fill up the brood chambers with winter stores.

Commercial comb honey producers crowd their colonies. The objective is to pack a large number of bees into a small space, then persuade them to make honeycomb, but refrain from swarming. No comb honey producer is 100 percent successful at that—or this one isn't, I must admit.

Combining the Brood Chambers

Wait until the early spring swarming season is past to make up a really productive comb honey colony. You must take apart a strong two-chamber hive. Put the ten best-filled brood frames into one chamber and store (freeze) honeycomb to return to them later in the year. Any excess brood can be distributed to weaker colonies. Then shake all the bees into a single hive body and put on an excluder and a super or two. The crowded bees will pour onto the foundation and begin drawing comb. Add and take off supers routinely, and add a super before the inner cover becomes too densely packed with bees.

High-output comb honey production takes close attention, and the books are full of complex manipulations that you can try. A main objective is to prevent your crowded colonies from swarming. The weekly swarm check is essential. The minute a honeyflow ceases, the colony has to go into stores for sustenance. This runs counter to instinct, and they will begin to think about swarming. In the home apiary, I feed the comb honey colonies through spells of bad weather.

Most important—don't skimp on supers. Foragers need inside roosting space at night, so supply excess comb rather than too little.

Using Comb Honey

The easiest way to distribute comb honey is whole and in the frame. Give or sell the entire frames as is and buy new frames.

For cut comb, remove and slice the comb into any size or shape you like from two-ounce single-serving bites to two-pound hunks. Drain them over a grid (an all-metal queen excluder makes a good drain), then pack them into plastic bags or the rigid plastic boxes sold by supply houses.

Odd shaped chunks (which is why it's called chunk honey) can be put into wide-mouthed peanut butter or pickle jars; and the jars topped with extracted honey. Pour it down the side of the jar to avoid entrapping bubbles.

Each section of the country has its preferred way of using comb honey—whole, cut, or chunk. I find that people like receiving gifts of an especially pretty piece of chunk comb in sparkling-clear liquid honey. The comb does encourage honey to crystallize, so package it just before giving or selling it, and warn users. (It will clear up after a bath in not-quite simmering water.)

To extract honey from small amounts of comb, have company handy to scratch your nose if need be, crush the comb in your hands, drain, and strain as with extracted. Or, you can stack combs and press them between boards if you have a cider press. Heated honey will flow nicely and you can strain small quantities through a kitchen strainer, then through cheesecloth to clarify as well as you like.

A decade ago, baby Martha watched from the bouncy chair as Louise cut a comb of honey from a half-depth frame.

These days the roles are reversed as Mom watches and Martha harvests the half-frames.

Squashing comb by hand is gooey, but the best way to make sure that all of the cells are ruptured.

The jar contains chunks of comb honey surrounded by crystal-clear liquid gold.

Sections

I have three rules for trying to produce honey sections, and they don't come with a recommendation. I won't try it unless I have:

1. **A really strong and vibrant colony that has already largely filled at least one conventional super with comb honey.**

2. **A real bell-ringer of a honeyflow, which means white clover around here in mid-July most years.**

3. **Time and inclination to sugar-feed the colony any time the honeyflow slackens (which would make my section honey adulterated and unsalable).**

Good Honeyflow Needed

If you have a strong and reliable and predictable honeyflow where you keep bees, sections may be for you. (I hope so; it is the most satisfying way to produce honey.) However, you'll need special hardware to hold the sections in modified supers, and must buy the section frames—all equipment sold in most of the catalogs.

I've given up (for now) on the lovely square basswood beeway sections, but am having some success with Ross Rounds (named after Tom Ross, who developed the equipment). These are plastic circles that come in a plastic framework at a cost of about $35 per super, complete and assembled. You can make up your own from a beeway section super plus about $8 worth of parts, $15 in plastic frames, and the little rings which are sold by the hundred for about $13. You must have the rings and plastic "Visi-Chek" frames. Conventional foundation slips fairly easily into the frames. This is a proprietary product and I'm not necessarily endorsing it for your use. But the frames do give the bees much more traveling space and they seem to enter the open round sections a little less hesitantly than the old-time squares that have nothing but a little slit for the bees to enter.

Also, for the market-oriented beekeeper, rounds lack the corners that bees are least happy to fill in any frame, and they hold about half the amount of honey as a square section—and often sell for more when packed in clean and modern looking plastic cups that come KD in four pieces, 200 to a box for 30 cents each.

Square sections are still sold in 1930ish-looking cardboard boxes where the comb peers out of skep-shaped cellophane windows that don't show the pretty and expensive section frame. These boxes come 100 to a carton for about 15 cents each.

A beeway section super costs $15 KD plus about $20 for 100 sections split so you can insert foundation. Then you need a splitting gadget to insert foundation and must assemble each of a super's thirty wood sections. Either section scheme is a lot of bother for a marketing device that gives the honey a never-touched-by-human-hands look. There's no way I know to get into section honey on a small scale or on the cheap, nor any way to produce it simply and consistently.

Encouraging the Bees

To encourage bees into sections, beekeepers use a variety of tricks. Some plant bait sections in the frames containing drawn comb or comb and honey from prior years. Others crowd the bees to the limit, without making them swarm.

Harvest is a snap; sections pop right out. Partly filled sections are used for chunk or returned as bait sections.

I love messing around with sections, am successful some years, but recommend that you wait until your second year to so much as consider them. And before you do, read Dr. Miller's *Fifty Years Among the Bees* to learn the old-time ways. Richard Taylor's *The*

New Comb Honey Book offers up-to-date techniques (including a photo of the comb honey-producer's complete kit of honey house equipment—a kitchen paring knife).

A Summary

To sum up, no matter what kind of honey production you may fancy, start out with conventional dual brood chamber colonies. You must decide, before adding the supers, whether you will extract or harvest the comb wax and all, since reinforced foundation is needed for extracting but not for comb honey. Extracting is the most complex harvest system, but will provide the greatest total return.

Combining a dual body colony into a single hive body for intensive comb or section honey production is a step that few first-year beekeepers should contemplate. Or, perhaps I should say, don't count on trying the advanced procedures the first year. But what if that especially productive colony has drawn comb in both brood chambers and is moving into a second super, and the field next door is about ready to burst into acres of orange blossom or buckwheat or sweet clover? Go on and give it a try, and have fun! Experimentation is the heart of beekeeping.

WHAT GOES INTO HONEY

It takes a forager from 100 to more than 1500 flower visits to fill her honey stomach with some 70 milligrams (85 percent of body weight) of nectar. On returning to the hive, she passes it off to one or more house bees. They spend the better part of a half-hour masticating it, working it like bubblegum, before taking it to an empty cell for storage and further drying.

With each passage through the bees, the enzyme invertase and other digesters are added. The complex (disaccharide) sugar source is **inverted** into the simple sugars dextrose and levulose plus over a dozen other sugars and small amounts of vitamins, minerals, and other good things, including "inhibine," the name given to a once-mysterious ingredient that gives honey an antibiotic property long recognized by folk medicine.

Modern analysis indicates that the bacteria-killing agents include a dozen or so mild acids and the common topical disinfectant (and hair bleach) hydrogen peroxide, made from glucose by the bee-produced enzyme glucose oxidase. Not many doctors carry honey in their black bags these days, but you might find it a useful emergency antiseptic some time. Spoilage is further discouraged by the high concentration of solids; moisture content is reduced to 20 percent or less from an original 50 percent or more as the workers masticate the nectar and the ventilating crew continually fans air through the hive. During a strong honeyflow, a large colony hums all night as thousands of bees fan away, evaporating nectar.

All this makes properly cured and capped honey a concentrated energy source that is relatively immune to spoilage from bacterial or yeast activity. However, if honey contains over 17 percent moisture it may ferment and if it contains over 19 percent it will. It can absorb water from the air, and unless you have access to a laboratory refractometer, you won't know if honey is cured. Rule of thumb: don't harvest uncapped honey from eastern colonies. In some areas of the West, low-moisture honey can be assured when most of a frame is capped; in some humid areas air-drying of frames is desirable. Ask locally for the rule.

You can store honey in a refrigerator at a constant temperature below 50° F to inhibit yeast formation, or heat extracted honey to a wax-melting 145° F for a half-hour to kill the yeast spores. Comb honey keeps well when frozen at 0° F, which also kills wax moth eggs and larvae.

Some honey will granulate. This means it will grow crystals which give it a grainy texture, cause dysentery in bees using it, and make it susceptible to fermentation. Sourwood and tupelo honeys never granulate; alfalfa honey can't be kept from it. Unfortunately, granulation is a problem where honey keeps best, at refrigerator temperatures. If your extracted honey granulates, heat it in a pan of hot but not boiling water until it reliquifies. Granulated comb honey is good for feeding bees, but not in the very early spring when it can cause dysentery. If you feed it in dry weather, be sure to supply water.

A Health Food?

For years honey was thought to be more easily digested than common sugar, thus good for diabetics, folks with digestive problems, and infants. Not so. "We have no evidence that honey is superior to sugar," says Dr. David Jenkins of the Department of Nutritional Sciences at the University of Toronto, in a 1985 interview with Times-Post News Service reporter Sally Squires. And, sugar is sugar—particularly to a diabetic. Most seriously, when fed in formula to babies under a year old, unsterilized honey has been implicated in the growth of dangerous pathogens in the baby's digestive system. The health food industry and some in the bee industry debate these findings, but I don't know a pediatrician who does. Human babies aren't bee larvae, and are no more built to handle the microbes or sugars or pollen in honey than little bees can handle breast milk or Pablum. Bees don't get diabetes or indigestion either.

Let's appreciate honey for what it is, a gloriously flavored and scented sweetener, just one gift from our bees. Another is the wax.

USING BEESWAX

The best use for your beeswax is comb honey to add crunch to the honey you put on the kids' toast. Next best use is to make new foundation. What's left over can be used to wax skis, lubricate sticking drawers, add flex to auto fan belts, and mold into the finest candles known.

We trade off about eight pounds of honey for each pound of wax. That's what it takes to fuel the bees' little wax factories. This figure comes from an experiment by W. Whitcomb, Jr., published in a 1946 issue of *Gleanings in Bee Culture*, and accepted still. With honey selling for about a half-dollar a pound wholesale these days, and the wax, which "costs" eight pounds of half-dollar honey to produce, selling for less than $2 per pound, it's small wonder that commercial bee people concentrate on extracted honey production and charge a premium price for the comb or section product. However, if you price pure handmade beeswax candles and factor in the fun of making them, home-produced beeswax is a fully economic product for the hobbyist.

It you extract, expect about a quarter-pound of capping wax per standard super. If you melt down entire shallow supers, as we do for the small amounts of liquid honey we need, expect perhaps a pound to a pound and a quarter of wax total. As I calculate it, that consists of more than ten ounces of thin foundation plus another five ounces of bee-produced comb and capping per ten-frame super. A fine pair of ten-inch tapers about ¾" at the base weighs four ounces and will light a month's worth of formal sit-down dinners at our place. If we make four sets of candles, thus four months of gentle illumination from a pound of wax, the three supers I can get from any one good colony in a decent year will light dinner the year through, and then some. We use the balance as gifts.

Working Up the Wax

The raw material for your wax will look like a mess of sticky cappings and pressed comb, burr and brace comb, and scrapings.

If you want to refine wax effortlessly, get a solar wax melter. You can make the one described later in the book for pocket change or buy it for $30–$40. It's a box, painted heat-absorbing black inside, with a clear plastic cover. Placed in the sun, its inside temperature will rise 100° or so above the air temperature, easily above the 145° F melting point of beeswax. You can pour the pure wax off, leaving behind the old cocoons, bee parts, and hive frass collectively termed slumgum, a wonderfully descriptive word. One caution: the residue can burn and the honey caramelize if left too long in the melter.

Cleaning the Wax

Your wax may be a deep brown from pollen and propolis stain. Commercial processors bleach it with chemicals that can't be recommended for home use. But you can stir it around in warm water, with some detergent or hydrogen peroxide added, to leach out most of the contamination.

A caution: beeswax will erupt in searing hot flame, not quite an explosion, but a real flare, if hot melted wax hits open flame or a red-hot electric heating coil. Water and wax don't mix, and even the small amount of water contained in pure wax can bubble into steam. Then it will roil up, throwing blobs of hot wax out of the pot. It's best to take the time to heat wax over water, double-boiler style. Don't use actively boiling water to clean it, and never leave the room when wax and a heat source are keeping company. Commercial processors use steam, heated at a remote location.

Storing the Wax

Once it is cleaned, you can pour the wax into paper milk cartons for storage. Or pour it into a pan, then cut it into bars like soap. If you like, you can sell your wax to the manufacturer for cash, trade it for beeware, or have it processed directly into foundation of any style you want.

I make my own thin, eating-style foundation from our own wax. Not that the commercial product isn't pure and clean; beeswax is beeswax. Maybe it's the challenge of making the equipment from scratch, since you can't buy a foundation press. When manufacturers can buy your wax for $2 a pound and return it to you pressed into foundation for $8, why should they sell foundation molds? See the photo series and join me if you care to. The home-pressed article isn't as elegant as the store-bought but the bees like it. You can start the frames in your shallow or section supers with just a top strip of home-pressed foundation. The bees will do the rest.

MAKING BEESWAX CANDLES

Pure beeswax candles are a luxury known to few and appreciated as a gift by everyone. A frame of perfect white-capped comb honey flanked by a pair of handmade beeswax tapers will endear you (and your bees) to any especially valued person on your holiday gift list. That's what I send to my Georgetown cousins who lunch with Henry Kissinger and those people.

Choosing the Wick

You need wicking to match your beeswax. A length of package-wrapping string or even honest baling twine won't do unless you want to set candle-making back 300 years and end up with crooked, charred wicks with those little red glowing ends that smolder and smell after the flame is extinguished so you have to snuff them out. (If you do use poor wick and snuff with your fingers, be sure to lick them well first to avoid a nasty burn.)

Martha dips the wicking in warm wax, then rolls it into a point. This makes it easier to thread the wick through the tip of the candle mold.

A generous squirt of Pam or another non-stick cooking lubricant is needed so the candle won't stick to the mold.

Martha holds pencils to keep the wicks centered in the mold while I pour the wax.

*Martha yanks the finished candles from the mold while Sam stands
ready to help.*

Modern self-snuffing wick is made of braided and treated
(pickled) cotton, and you should buy the correct size. Too fat a wick
for the candle's wax formulation and width will smoke and gutter or
cause wasteful dripping. If too small, it will drown out in the little
cup of melted wax formed at the candle top. You've probably experienced both problems with inexpensive supermarket tapers or
amateur-made ornamentals.

Because beeswax burns more slowly than paraffin, it needs a
larger wick. The bleached cotton "square braid" is best for beeswax.
Flat braid is for paraffin and mixed waxes. There are at least 100
wick sizes, not all suited to beeswax. Many are described in candle-
making books. Sizes 0.1 and up the $\frac{1}{10}$ scale are for elegant, thin-
dipped candles and are too small for our brand of small-scale can-
dlemaking. Over the years we've picked up some No. 1 square-
braided wick for rolled candles and No. 3 for larger tapers, plus several odd lengths of cored wick for those big fat gift-type candles that
burn down inside a hollow core. You can find wick at arts and crafts
suppliers and hobby shops. If they don't have it in stock, they can
order you some. The major U.S. manufacturer is Atkins & Pearce
Mfg. Co., 537 E. 2nd St., Cincinnati, OH 45202. This company sells
it mainly in reel lots, but offers samples for about $20.

Rolled Candles

Your first batch of wax will probably be pretty scant, and you may be tempted to flesh it out a little. Don't use the paraffin you buy to cap your strawberry jam. It has a high oil content, almost melts in your hand, and makes too soft a candle.

You'll find hard candle paraffin where you buy your wick, and a 51–49 beeswax/paraffin mix will qualify as a beeswax candle on most folks' dinner table.

There are other additives you may want to experiment with, especially if you add in a lot of paraffin. Stearic acid (two teaspoons per pound of wax) adds strength and opacity, and makes it easy to remove the candles from molds. You can mix dyes and scents and dream up all kinds of inclusions to go inside, and interesting textured stuff to put on the outside to add a wonderful variety to paraffin candles. But beeswax tapers, straight and simple, can't be improved upon.

The only way to eke a first year's harvest of a few ounces of wax into candles is to melt it, then pour it on a shallow pan of hot water where it will spread out. When it cools, you can remove it and make a rolled candle. Melt your wax over hot water, double-boiler style, never over direct flame.

After pouring it on the hot water, let it cool enough to handle. You'll remove it too warm once or twice, and it'll slump all over your hands, and then you'll wait too long so it cracks. But don't worry. Wax can be remelted forever and the knack and proper timing will come with experience.

A sun-warmed marble slab kitchen counter is best for candle rolling, as it is for sticky-candy making. Lacking one, we put the sheets on a Teflon cookie sheet that can be kept warm on a stove top.

Trim the wax to a rectangle, or angle the top for a taper. Place a length of wick longer at each end than the wax sheet along the long edge. Then roll the sheet up slowly, smoothing between thumb and forefinger as you go. The final taper is thinned and smoothed at the top by rolling on the flat surface, then straightened by pulling on each end of the wick.

To prevent the inevitable bending as the candle cools, hang it from the top length of wick and tie a weight on the bottom end. It may still arch a little as it burns, adding proof if you need it that the candle is handmade.

Dipping and Molding

Candle-dipping is a great old-time skill, but it takes gallons of beeswax, more than most hobby beekeepers will collect.

We've never had enough wax on hand to try it, to be honest, and I refer you to the books in the appendix for information.

More appropriate for the small-scale beekeeper is to make candles from molds. You can find genuine antiques for a price, or you can buy reproductions from a few mail order stores and retail sources. Dr. Robert Berthold, Jr., Delaware Valley College, Doylestown, PA 18901, knows bees and beeswax and sells reasonably priced, antique-design tin candle-making molds by mail.

Coat the inside of the molds with a thin layer of vegetable oil or one of those anti-stick sprays. Handmade candles are made in pairs on a single length of wick and are joined at the tip end if dipped, at their bases if molded. String the wick ends through the tip end of adjacent molds by wrapping the wick around flexible wire already pushed up into the mold. Hold it taut and centered in each tube by cinching the end protruding from the bottom around straws or clamping between hairpins.

Place the tip end on a wet cloth or sponge and pour a small bit of wax in each tube tip. Let it firm up a bit to seal the end. Then pour in the wax slowly to let air escape without bubbling and spattering hot wax out on your hands. Beeswax shrinks as it cools, so you'll have to top up several times. Don't overflow the top or you'll never get the candles out.

The filled mold can be plunged into cold water to hasten cooling. Wax will shrink from the mold, and the candles should slide right out. If they don't, immerse them in hot water and apply gentle pressure until they come out.

WAX FACTS

Beeswax is a remarkable formulation of more than 300 hydrocarbons, esters, and acids. When formed into the bee's spectacular architecture, wax comb can support more than 1,000 times its own weight, though typical comb contains one pound of wax for each twenty pounds of honey. Essentially inert, wax lasts as near to forever as life substance can. Wax refined to royal purity found in the Egyptian kings' tombs remains as white and sweet and

pliant as when interred thousands of years ago.
Beeswax candles will maintain their shape at temperatures above 110° F, when paraffin candles slump. The wax becomes ductile and workable at about 97° F, melts at 143° to 151°, which is well below the boiling point of water, burns at 400° F, but has a high flashpoint of about 500° F. This means that it is a little slow to ignite, but burns hot and clean and for a long time, and with a faint honey scent that seems to cleanse the air.

Production

The bee colony is stimulated to produce wax by two influences operating in concert:

1. **The prospect of full honey crops all around.**
2. **No drawn comb to store it in.**

These can also encourage swarming. However, if weather is warm, nectar taken from foragers or a well-received sugar-syrup feeder has the house bees filled to overflowing, and if the beekeeper has destroyed queen cells and added a super in enough time to preclude the swarming urge, some bees will cease working and hang locked together quietly in bee garlands or festoons, all their energy going into wax glands beneath the four pairs of rear lower abdominal scales.

Wax is emitted as successive fluid layers that harden into laminated flakes which begin to extrude from under the scales in two or three days. Bees pull each flake back and out with their hind legs, chew it up, and apply it to new comb.

If foundation is introduced at the right time, the bees will immediately begin to draw comb from the supplied wax, augmenting it with their own as produced. My experience suggests they increase the twenty ounces of wax in each standard frame hive box with some ten ounces of their own to produce the two pounds of wax we obtain from a carefully harvested standard hive body. A new swarm or well-motivated strong colony can draw two frame sides overnight and will complete most of a standard hive body in a week of warm weather.

Wax From Old Comb

It's a matter of pride for North American beekeepers to continue using old comb. Some express considerable pride in exhibiting comb their grandfathers used, still in production after fifty years, though black as pitch and greatly reduced in capacity. Workers clean and polish a cell after each new bee emerges, but they don't remove the cocoons, which slowly build up and reduce inner dimensions of the cell. This results in smaller bees with less strength and carrying capacity. In one observation, the weight of bees fell from 118 milligrams for workers raised in normal cells to 96 milligrams for the sixty-eighth generation in the same cells. That's almost a 20 percent reduction. This is one reason why European beekeepers melt down their comb after three or four years. They also feel that the old, dark comb stains honey. That's a debatable point. The queen prefers dark comb, the older the better apparently, and old comb is best for hiving swarms and retaining swarm-prone colonies that lack empty comb or reject foundation. I've never had to discard comb. It becomes damaged in handling or gets too full of drone cells or chewed up before I ever have to worry about its years in use.

MAKING A FOUNDATION PRESS

The only press for making beeswax foundation that I've ever seen for sale is a beautifully made cast metal, giant waffle iron type of press from England. It costs a bundle. Mine is handmade from scrap lumber and hardware store goods, was put together over a weekend, and cost $6.68 plus 33 cents sales tax for the matrix materials needed to make the dies. Lumber, hinges, glue, and nails were lying around the place, but might have added another $3 bought new. Put the cost at $10. That's less than the price of two loads of shallow foundation.

The press consists of a pair of heavy blocks a bit larger all around than a sheet of foundation, framed in wood, and hinged on the long side so the halves close together much like a long, narrow book. Inside, where the halves meet, are a pair of dies, castings taken from a sheet of beeswax foundation. To make foundation, you pour hot wax onto the die face of one half, then close the press quickly to distribute wax evenly between the dies. When the wax is cooled, you open the press and remove a sheet of homemade foundation.

The lateral dimensions of the frame need only be a little bigger around than the foundation size you prefer. I make shallow eating foundation for comb honey, so the press is twenty inches long and eight inches wide. To make standard size foundation, increase the width to ten inches. Each side of my press is about one inch deep, enough to hold nearly ten pounds of matrix.

Materials and Tools

- 2 lengths 20″×2″×1″ finished lumber
- 2 lengths 8″×2″×1″ finished lumber
- 2 24″×6″ lengths of window screening
- 2 dozen large nails (10 penny)
- 1 dozen 1½″ finish nails
- 1 pair of sturdy butt-type hinges
- 1 box fine-grained, hard cold-curing matrix (artist's casting mix, dental stone, or water putty)
- 1 box plaster of paris
- 1 piece foundation
- Wax paper
- Staple gun and ½″ staples
- Mortar mix (portland cement and sand) to make 20 pounds
- Carpenter's glue
- Mixing pail
- Saw
- Hammer
- Paintbrush
- Work table

Making the Press

To make the frames, split down the middle the 1″×2″ lumber into four 20″ and four 8″ strips, each about 1″×1″.

Cut the corners of each piece at 45° angles, then make the two frames, using glue and nails to hold the pieces together. I used 1½″ finish nails, but any nail 1″ or longer will do; the frame itself doesn't have to be particularly sturdy, since it will be filled with the solid matrix. When the glue is dry, staple one end of a length of the window screen into the inside of each frame at one end, and tap large nails inside all four sides of each frame. The screen and nails will hold the matrix in the frame.

FOUNDATION PRESS

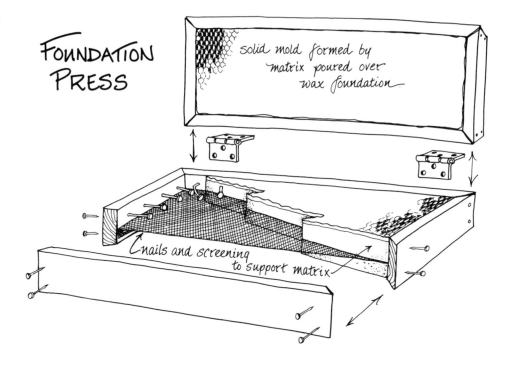

solid mold formed by matrix poured over wax foundation

nails and screening to support matrix

Cut a piece of wax paper that will just fit inside one frame. Place a frame on your work table, fit the piece of wax paper inside it, then place the beeswax foundation on top of the wax paper. That foundation will form the positive impression to be molded.

Your next step will be to fill the frame with three layers of materials, mixing each according to package directions and allowing each to dry before the next one is applied. Put them on in this order.

1. A thin layer of hard-setting water putty. This goes over the wax foundation to form the face of the die that will make the mold for the new foundation. This is the most expensive material, so the least is used. Don't try epoxy or other mastics that heat while curing. I tried this, and found they melt the wax enough to obliterate essential detail.

When the drying matrix becomes tacky as it dries, press the window screen into it, and staple the free end to the inside of the frame at the other end. This screen will provide needed reinforcement for the dies, so work it well into the matrix.

The wood strips are held together with glue and nails.

The window screen reinforcement is stapled onto one end of the first frame. Note the nails hammered into the wood to hold the main body of the matrix.

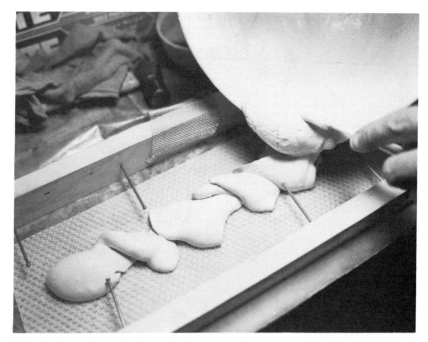

With the foundation in place, the fine-grained matrix is poured in.

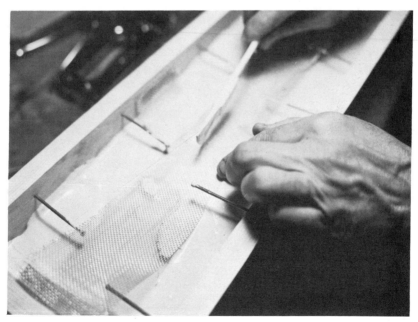

Screen is pressed into the matrix, then stapled to the other end.

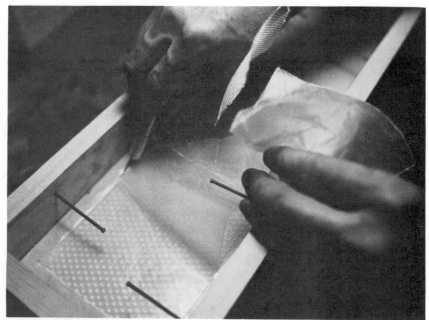

A mask of wax paper is put around the wax foundation being used as a master mold pattern to keep the matrix from sticking to non-wax surfaces.

When the molds are completed, their faces are painted with a thin coat.

2. A layer of plaster of paris to bond to the matrix. This is a cheaper but still fine-grained material that will squash down through the window screen reinforcement with gentle kneading. It is hard to mix, though, and it sets quickly, so you have to pour it in quickly. Don't answer the telephone in mid-pour.

3. A heavy matrix, to fill the mold to the rim. I used ready-mix portland cement-based mortar that I had on hand. You can fill the form with such a mortar, with plaster of paris, or even with water putty.

When this first frame is dry, invert it, and join it to the second frame with the hinges. Remove the wax paper and chip away any matrix that intruded on the wax.

Using wax paper, cut a mask that will fit around a sheet of foundation. Place this mask around the foundation that is still on the first frame. Don't oil the wax of the foundation to improve the parting of the mold halves. It will bubble the cast—as I learned by trying it.

Close the press. Now with the press on the work table and the empty frame on top, fill that frame just as you did the first frame, layer by layer, letting each dry before adding the next one.

After the matrixes are poured into the second half and dried, gently pry the frames open. Take off the wax paper mask and the foundation used as a mold. You may have to chip off some matrix around the edges, but the wax should have left strong impressions in each half of the mold. If some of the wax is stuck to one side of the mold, pour boiling water over the mold faces. The wax will melt and flow away.

Dry the foundation press and paint the faces of the dies with polyurethane varnish (hard-gloss finish). Brush this in well, but don't use too much or it will mask detail of the mold. I used a super-hard, clear floor paint, but any color will do.

Making Foundation

First, melt beeswax over hot water, not directly over a flame or burner, and keep it there except when pouring. I use an old tin pan that lost its handle long since for melting wax for both foundation and candles. A little butter-clarifying pan is a good hot wax dipper, and the cooktop of a fine old wood-cooking/heating range is unsurpassed for keeping the wax at a good pouring temperature. Steps in making the foundation follow.

1. Spray a light coat of vegetable (edible) cooking lubricant such as Pam on both dies of the foundation press, and wipe off all excess. Bees don't like foundation that tastes of anything but honey

First, paint the dies and wood frames with Pam so wax won't stick.

Pour the hot wax in as perfect a sheet as you can. Then close the press.

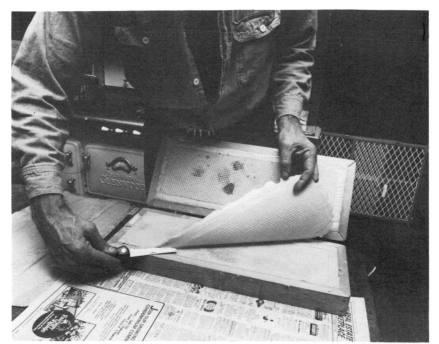

Pry the press open with a knife. You may have to tease the edges of the wax sheet up from the frames.

Trim off the excess wax.

And here is the sheet of wax foundation, from your own bees.

or beeswax. Pour hot wax rapidly on the dished face of the first mold you made, in as near a sheet as possible. Pour it on fast and do not worry about wax slopping over.

2. Close the press. Slam it shut for the thinnest foundation, if you don't mind splatter. Press down hard to squirt the wax out into a sheet. Some wax will dribble out of the front and sides of the mold. Return it to the melt.

3. Let the wax cool. When the translucent hot-wax color of the sheet changes to opaque, loosen the edges, open the press, and peel off the new foundation. Trim wax overflow from around the edges. Store the finished foundation between sheets of paper you saved from bought foundation, or use wax paper.

To obtain a uniform, well-impressed sheet of foundation, you must pour the wax and close the press quickly. It takes a little practice, and the foundation will vary in thickness and will never be as perfect as the machine-made. But you'll have foundation from wax produced by your own bees, who will take to it as well as the commercial variety and maybe better.

A sheet of commercial thin, eating foundation for a shallow super contains about a half-ounce of wax. I've never been able to squeeze a sheet from so little; most of my sheets weigh up to four times as much. To allow for slop, I have a little more wax on hand than is needed for the foundation itself, or 2½ ounces per sheet. That's about 1½ pounds of wax for ten frames of shallow super-sized eating foundation and a good two pounds to make up a ten-frame lot of full-sized foundation.

If your early wax harvests are limited, you can melt down commercial foundation or buy block wax from any equipment supplier. Don't be tempted to use paraffin or anything but pure beeswax; bees are choosy.

To stretch a thin wax harvest, you'll find that a 1½-inch strip of foundation put in at the top of a frame will get the bees working, and they'll build it down to the bottom in no time. By cutting my own 5-inch wide foundation into three strips, I can get bees working in a super with only a third the wax that would be needed for a super filled with full-size homemade foundation.

Wire-reinforced Foundation

To embed wires in homemade foundation, scratch out grooves in the sides and bottom of the borders of each die and the frame itself for the wires to stick out. Make the grooves a bit smaller than the wire so it can be held tight and straight as the mold is being made. Drill nine or ten evenly spaced small holes at the top of one die face to hold the 90° bent ends of the vertical wires. Then cut soft wire (the kind that doesn't curl or kink) to length for both horizontal and vertical supports (or salvage crimped and hook-ended wire from old foundation).

The bottom of the verticals and end of each of the four horizontal wires should be a few inches longer than the frame so they can be pulled tight as the wax hardens, and so the horizontals may be tightened once the foundation is installed in the frame.

Lay the wires in place. You may have to hold protruding ends of wires with a weight to keep them in place before closing the mold. I use old bricks. You can put a drop of hot wax into the holes/grooves that contain each wire, imbed the wires in it and let cool to hold the wires in place as the wax goes in.

Then pour the hot wax and close the press. Pull protruding ends of wires tight immediately, and let the foundation harden before you remove it.

Installing Prewired Foundation into Frames

To install wired foundation in a frame, bow the foundation enough to push ends of horizontals through the holes in the frame side pieces. Place the hooked ends of the verticals under the frame wedge as usual. Then tighten the horizontals by twisting adjacent top and bottom pairs of wire together with pliers until the wires are tight. Don't twist the wires so tight you split the frame ends. Clip off excess wire, then turn the twist connections and press them into the wood of the end piece so they won't interfere with frame removal.

A SOLAR WAX MELTER

A wax melter fueled by the sun is a traditional beekeeping appliance. The power is free, the procedure needs no supervision, and the burnable wax is rendered and cleaned without getting close to open flame.

Beeswax needs only 145° F to melt, so the temperature rise is moderate and easily reached in a double-glazed, insulated box exposed to direct sunlight.

Pennsylvania State University publishes a dandy design, several beebooks contain plans for other build-it-yourself models, and you can buy melters readymade from the larger suppliers. These are too large for most backyard apiaries, and making one that size takes considerable skill.

My solar wax melter is made from a paint-roller tray. It fits nicely into a dark, heat-absorbing ¾-sized (Dadant) super. I tacked on a plywood bottom and lined this super-box with rigid plastic house-insulating foam. I used two sheets of hardware store plastic window glazing. You can use any depth hive body or make a box from scratch. Glass would be better insulation than the plastic I used. The foam is cut to fit and pressed into place with no fasteners needed, so the super can be used again in a hive by pulling out the insulation and prying off the bottom.

I fastened the window plastic together in an airtight sandwich with ¼" wooden strips between, then fastened it all together with epoxy glue and brads. One sheet of plastic fits into the frame rests and the other covers the entire top.

The roller tray is fitted with short legs at the top (shallow) end. The well end rests in a small teflon-coated tray. A piece of half-inch hardware cloth crimped onto the sloped surface of the roller tray serves to hold the wax as it melts and to catch most of the slumgum, and a wooden dam is epoxied into the top end of the well to hold the rest. It allows the wax to trickle over as it melts. I drilled holes in the wax-catching end of the well bottom so hot wax can dribble into the little baking tray below.

Put the melter in full sun, then toss in chunks of old comb and let it heat. Keep adding comb until either the slumgum catch tray or the wax pan is nearly full. It's tidier to do wax in small batches and clean the tray right after the wax melts, or the honey will caramelize and make an awful mess. Any honey that is heated to wax-melting temperatures will be off-flavored and should be discarded. It shouldn't even be fed back to the bees.

Martha paints the inside of the box with flat black paint. The paint tray is also painted black.

Wax comb is placed in the melter.

When the two layers of plastic are put over the top, the interior quickly heats up to wax-melting temperatures.

When the wax has melted, it's easy to pour it off.

Chapter 7

SLOW MONTHS
AND
SECOND SPRING

As summer winds down, honeyflows dwindle, and darkness comes sooner, the bees prepare the hive for winter. The eager pace of comb building and egg production slows as hive population diminishes by slow attrition to less than half the spring peak.

Even the bees are different. Winter bees eat more pollen protein than spring bees, and are capable of surviving up to six months in the winter cluster.

The drone population declines, too, as mating season ends. You've doubtless read of worker bees pushing drones from the hive to die in the fall chill. This sounds cruel and heartless, but it's a fact of beelife. Indeed, if you notice many drones or capped drone cells in a hive from late summer on, it indicates a failed or failing queen. She, too, must go.

They Don't Hibernate

Honeybees originated in the tropics, so they don't hibernate the winter away like most cold-blooded creatures native to our own climate. As day temperatures cool and brood rearing slows, bees prepare for winter in the hive bodies left to them. As temperatures fall below 57° F, the bees will cluster, and until brood rearing resumes, adult bees will occupy empty cells as well as intercomb space. The queen will stay near the center, constantly fed and serviced by her attendants. The cluster moves slowly over the combs as stores are consumed, expanding on warmer days and contracting on cooler ones to maintain the outer perimeter of the mass at about 45° F no matter how cold the outside air.

The colony retains a low activity level, but the bees are perfectly alert and capable of flying on any warm day. In the South, bees will forage when weather permits. In the North, they can be socked in by cold rains in November, not to see daylight again until May. Even if the world outside the hive is frozen solid and the snow is six feet deep in the apiary, come late winter the queen will begin laying eggs on brood comb maintained at 93° to 95° F by a 1"-to-3" blanket of heat-producing and insulating workers. You must assure in advance that stores are sufficient, hives are sound and dry, colony numbers adequate, and queens vigorous. Up to half the colony will expire naturally over a hard winter, but no bee will freeze or starve so long as the beekeeper does his part.

Stores

Your first priority is to make sure the bees have adequate food. If colonies starve, it's almost always when the early brood-raising period of late winter and early spring places new demands on food supply. That's often after bees are bringing in early pollen and nectar, so the beekeeper assumes all is well. The rule of thumb suggested by most experts for commercial hives that will receive little attention until spring is to assure that colonies have twenty pounds of honey over minimum needs. If you're like I am after a winter's gloom, you will be positively panting for a sunny February day when you can inspect the apiary and provide feed if needed. So, your colonies won't really need the insurance—though it can't hurt. Minimum stores for a colony in the South that can forage year-round are only about twenty pounds of stored honey and very little pollen. In the North, the same bees would need ninety pounds of honey and 500 square inches of pollen to be in top shape for the sudden and powerful spring honeyflow. A North American average range is thirty to sixty pounds of honey (five to ten full frames) and the equivalent of two full frame faces of pollen.

Factors in Food Consumption

Your winter management scheme plays a crucial role in stores planning. Bees wintered outside in uninsulated hives in cold climates will pack together, maintaining a low metabolic rate and using fewer stores than the same bees that could be more active in a warmer locale. But they may not loosen their cluster enough to move and can starve only one empty frame away from food. Cold starvation, it's called.

Bees kept inside a dark building where temperatures are around 40°, but constant, will cluster loosely and be able to reach food easily, and won't need as much food as bees in fluctuating, colder temperatures outdoors. The indoor colonies usually can manage on stores contained in a single hive body, while outdoors they would need a second story.

Be Generous

It's best to err on the generous side though. Leave or give extra food and be sure not to make the mistake common to new beekeepers and harvest off the bees' own honey (though you can return it to them through fall or spring feeding, see below).

I have a simple rule that works for me in the Northeast. When the wild flowers turn yellow, when goldenrod replaces the white of clover and Queen Anne's lace and the blue of wild asters and chicory along the roadsides, I quit taking supers of honey unless it's truly superfluous to the bees' own. I leave a super containing partly filled or brood-sprinkled honeycomb frames above the single brood chamber of each productive comb honey colony beginning in mid to late August. The queen excluder and any added supers are placed above this, and if the queen uses the first super for brood for a while, that's good; bees prefer to winter on used brood comb. They will pack brood chamber and super with their fall honey, which is often bitter.

If you have dual brood chambers, switch them in late summer, putting the top one on the bottom, and leave winter nest arrangement and storage to the bees.

Have Hives Inspected

Now is a good time to make an important telephone call, to the local bee inspector. Any area beekeeper, equipment retailer, or county agent will have the number. Make an appointment to have your colonies inspected, and politely ask the inspector if he sterilizes his hive tool, gloves, and any equipment that will touch your hives after encountering American foulbrood. The good ones do, all should, and if yours doesn't, insist that he use your tools. Not even forty years' beekeeping experience will keep contaminated equipment from spreading AFB spores from hive to hive.

Go with him as your apiary is checked. Be prepared for the loss of a colony if AFB is present, though the chances are slight. The inspector's experienced eye can help judge colony strength and pick out other problems you may have overlooked. He'll also know of any disease in the area, equipment going up for sale, and other beekeepers with knowhow to share. You can also ask his expert advice on wintering requirements in your locale.

Disease Prevention and Culling

If there is no farm or veterinary supply outlet nearby, look through the catalogs and order a supply of Fumidil B for nosema treatment now, and again next spring, and some Terramycin to feed in the fall and spring against the foulbroods. Neither medication will kill spores, but they will prevent the pathogens from developing when the colony is most susceptible.

You can medicate with Fumidil B in an inside-the-hive syrup feeder. Terramycin may be supplied dry or in syrup, but is unstable in an aqueous solution when exposed to sunlight, so should never be fed in a glass entrance feeder. It comes in a variety of concentrations for different applications, so follow directions to supply a quarter to a half gram of the active ingredient to each colony. Offer it mixed in a gallon or two of sugar syrup in fall supplementary feeding, or stir it into a box of confectioner's powdered sugar and sprinkle it on the frame tops or inner cover, or supply it in a dry feeder. Wait until the harvest is well past and bees are packing away the fall nectar for their own winter stores before medicating. Dosages will be found on the packages, and more detail is included in Chapter 9.

Check the Hives

A careful late-season hive overhaul and culling is in order, too. Be sure there are no cracks in hive bodies, tops, or bottoms to admit winter winds. Scrape bottom boards well and examine the scrapings for mites. If bottom boards are wet, improve your hive bases or move hives a foot or two at a time into a drier, sunnier area. Be sure the hives will receive full sun in the winter, particularly in the North. If possible, remove any undrawn foundation and replace it with drawn comb or honeycomb. If, as sometimes happens with package bees that don't develop well, all frames in the brood chamber aren't drawn by late summer, begin stimulative feeding and plan to replace the queen. In later years, you'll probably divide a weak colony's bees and stores among stronger colonies.

Find the queen if you can easily. She should be plump, active, and well-attended. Her laying pattern should still be good and tight, though capped brood will be found on fewer combs. If you find spotty brood or many drones, plan to requeen. Ditto if you find swarm or supersedure cells; it may be too late in the season for a newly emerging queen to perform a normal spring function—to fly and mate successfully—and she would be a drone-layer for sure.

End of Season Requeening

Many bee experts recommend replacing queens at the end of every season, or at least after two years. Queens can live for five or more years, but that is extremely rare. No one knows how long queens survive in nature. (They would head successive swarms as they form new colonies year after year.) But in an apiary, colonies naturally supersede their queen more frequently than we realize, often more than once a year. With each supersedure you are losing the good characteristics so carefully reselected by the professional breeder who supplied your original queens.

You may find it cruel to pluck your queen off her comb, kill her, and install a foreign queen, but you are only managing a process that takes place naturally all the time. If your queen has produced exceptionally well her first year, by all means keep her for another season. But requeening is the best guarantee of a good honey supply in following years. Honeybee queens produce the most and best eggs and exert the strongest chemical control over their colonies their first season. A young queen will be full of youthful vitality and nest-building instinct. Her chances of surviving the winter and initiating strong brood production in spring are greater than a queen's who has a full season or more behind her.

You don't want a queen to fail or die in late fall or during the winter when there are no fresh, fertilized (female) eggs to be raised into a new queen. A failed queen will be unable to initiate strong brood raising in spring, and may even be unable to fertilize her eggs, becoming a drone layer. Her colony is doomed unless the beekeeper discovers the situation and requeens before overwintered workers begin to expire in the spring.

Death of A Queen

When a queen dies and the hive senses the loss of her chemical dominance, colony morale and organization falter within a half-hour. Bees act nervous and the colony will be grumpy. Within a few hours, workers begin constructing emergency supersedure cells, and they won't settle down until chemical balance is restored by a new queen. In a few days more the vestigal ovaries and attached plumbing in some workers begin to develop and will continue unless the pheromones of a new queen reexert control over the colony.

Lacking a new queen, these laying workers begin producing eggs. One may even develop into a false queen, with enlarged abdomen and just enough pheromones to attract a coterie of attendants.

However, laying workers scatter eggs around the hive in random clumps attached to cell sides rather than the neat single eggs at the bottoms of adjacent cells that distinguish the work of a good queen. Unfertilized, the laying worker eggs that develop become small drones. Often, laying worker brood is permitted to die and rot. The result is most unpleasant.

DON'T INTERFERE WITH SUPERSEDURE

In any season, natural mortality (or more commonly, beekeeper incaution during an inspection) can kill a queen. The dead queen has provided the last of her viable fertilized eggs to rear her replacement. If you remove the supersedure cells, you may create a laying worker colony. Also, supersedure is often started when a perfectly good queen is laying well, but is abandoned in mid-process. Be on the safe side and respect the bees' instinct.

Remember the old TV advertising slogan: "Don't fool around with Mother Nature"? Well, it applies to honeybee supersedure. When it is going, let it go, until you have a reliable replacement queen to give the colony.

Requeening

I resisted requeening for years, believing the natural way was best. But, after several seasons of disappointing production, I've taken to requeening all but the most vigorous colonies. (And, if the first spring check indicates that a colony under an overwintered queen isn't fairly exploding with new brood, I get a new queen for that one, too.)

The first step is to order the new queen. When she arrives, you have three options, depending on the queen situation in your colony and on your own beekeeping intuition:

1. If a colony has been queenless for any time, install the new queen immediately. Some experts advise to soak her with sugar water and just dump her in the colony. Presumably the colony is so eager to become queenright, the term for a colony that has a queen,

The hive tool points to a cluster of emergency supersedure queen-raising cells. These are capped within a week of emerging. The beekeeper should not interfere with supersedure unless he has a new queen ready to give the colony and is willing to find and remove the old queen and to search the colony completely for queen cells that must be removed. If you do this, look again for queen cells after another week.

When your new queens arrive, open the envelope immediately and give them and their attendants a drink of room-temperature water. If you can't introduce them to the hive immediately, put them in a cool place and supply water twice a day. The candy plug in the cage will feed them for several days.

they will accept her immediately. (Be sure to put her in without the attendants who accompanied her in the shipping cage; they would cause trouble.) I've never tried this approach and don't trust it.

2. Introduce the queen in her shipping cage the same way you introduced the queen to the package bees last spring. I prefer this approach for a queenless colony. I've been told that you can use it to requeen a queenright colony, and that the young queen will search out and probably kill the old queen. I'm not convinced.

3. The most foolproof method of requeening is to make up a separate temporary colony. Put the queen in her cage in a separate nuc or brood box with two to four frames of bees and brood from the intended colony just as you did when you installed your package bees. Be sure the old queen isn't on these frames. Foragers moved will return to the parent hive, and house bees will accept a new queen happily. Put the nuc on top of the parent hive for a week or until the new queen is accepted and laying well. Then find the old queen, remove her, and put the new box on top of the old one with nothing but two folded sheets of newspaper between them. Cut several slits in the paper. Put covers on top of the dual-bodied colony, and wait.

In the few days it takes the bees to gnaw through the paper barrier, the distinct colony odors will mingle, and there should be no fighting. The new queen will be eagerly accepted by the newly queenless bees, and your combined colony is off to a new start. If all the paper isn't removed in a few more days, pull it out before it becomes propolized onto the frames.

Choose the system that you like. I prefer the paper-introduction method. It takes longer and is more bother, but we are doing something that isn't in nature's book, and I prefer the slow route.

Combining and Splitting Colonies

The paper system outlined above is the best way to combine colonies, such as making one good colony from two inferior ones. Forager bees will be lost when their home is moved, but will drift to other hives nearby. Don't just put one queenright colony on top of another with paper in between and expect the better of the two queens to win out in the inevitable battle to the death. The tougher of the two may be exhibiting feral characteristics that are an advantage in the wild, but unsuitable to an apiary. (This is an increasing possibility as the killer bees, or Africanized honeybees, colonize wild colonies in the southern areas of North America.)

Before combining two queenright colonies, search out and dispose of the inferior queen. Queens are not programmed to sting anything but competing queens, so you can just pluck one off the comb. The British suppliers listed at the end of this book sell dandy little plastic queen catchers that I find indispensable.

I let the poorer colony remain queenless for twenty-four hours, then install it over two sheets of newspaper on top of the better colony. After several days, the colony odors will have intermingled and brood frames of the colonies can be combined in the lower bee boxes. Here, too, foragers from the hive that was moved will be lost to the new combined colony, but will find homes by drifting among other colonies in your apiary.

These photos show a difficult cold, rainy season hive-split/requeening job. The original colony was started on foundation from a small wild swarm, but proved to have an uninspiring queen, so drew little comb. None of the other colonies could spare much brood comb or many bees so I had to scrounge for a starter colony to give the new queen. Weather was chilly, so I installed them in a nuc rather than a full-sized hive body to retain as much warmth as possible around the new queen and the few frames I could spare to give her and the new colony.

1. A frame of bees on partly drawn foundation goes into the nuc. Note the queen cage awaiting introduction hanging on one of two kinds of artificial comb foundation leaning against the nuc.

2. With three frames partly filled with bees installed, in goes the queen. The artificial comb will be added later (and, in this case at least, will be ignored by the bees).

3. After several days of rain, during which I fed both colonies with entrance feeders, and with the nuc that will hold the new queen waiting on the hive in the background, I searched for the failed queen.

4. *After the old queen has been removed from the colony, I laid two thicknesses of newspaper atop the hive. A series of small cuts is made in the paper so the two colonies' odors can intermingle slowly.*

5. *Since the nuc is smaller than the standard hive body, I put a board at each side of the hive. As still more rain was expected during the next week, I put a sheet of plastic between boards and paper, with the center cut out so the bees could intermingle through the paper.*

6. *Finally, I placed the nuc with the new queen on the hive body.*
After several days, I put frames from the nuc into the full-sized hive
body, and removed the paper, plastic, and boards.

Colony Division

Splitting especially strong colonies is a natural way to increase
the apiary and, in spring, to control swarming at the same time.
With the cost of package bees rising and the threat of Africanization
ever present, colony division will probably become a universal
practice. There are as many ways to do it as beekeepers. We covered padgening earlier. That is, moving a colony and putting a
newly hived swarm into its location so field bees will join the swarm.
In the parent colony, emerging brood will support the new queen.

Lacking a swarm, the way I usually divide is to order a new
queen, then, when she arrives, introduce her as with a package to
a new ten-frame brood body containing from two to four frames of
sealed brood with covering bees from a strong colony, being sure
the queen is not on the removed frames. Frames in both hives are
filled with foundation. If the source colony is boiling over with
young bees, I will shake bees off several honey frames to further
augment the new colony, which must be fed as a new package until
its foragers mature. You can make up colonies under a new queen
using frames and bees from several colonies. Brood bees won't fight,
and any bees of trouble-making, forager age will return to the parent

hive after their first trip out. I make up such a mixed-strain colony in the evening, leaving them queenless overnight. The next morning, I introduce the new queen in her shipping cage, still plugged with candy.

WINTER PREPARATIONS

Only with experience can you tell a colony's winter honey supply by simply hefting the winter hive, as commonly recommended. I still count frames. A packed standard frame contains about five pounds of honey. If your bees have honey in the three outer frames on each side of the brood chamber, that's $6 \times 5 = 30$ pounds, plenty to hold a normal-sized colony until the first late winter/early spring inspection in a mild climate. If they have filled a shallow super for an added thirty pounds, they'll have the sixty pounds that will carry any colony through to spring anywhere below Hudson Bay. A second standard hive body will provide a total of up to 100 pounds, enough for the longest winter.

Cross-section of
A WELL-PROVISIONED
WINTER HIVE:

- HONEY
- POLLEN (under a honey cap)
- POLLEN

Late Feeding

If the bees haven't put up sufficient stores as days begin to cool in early fall, you should begin fall feeding. Using an in-hive feeder to preclude robbing, feed a syrup of two parts sugar to one part water. Three five-pound sacks of sugar dissolved in one gallon of boiling water makes a convenient lot. With less brood to raise, bees use this syrup more efficiently than the weaker spring 1:1 mix, and will pack away eleven pounds of honey for each ten pounds of sugar you supply.

I've never heard of doing this, but even if you had to feed the bee's entire winter store of sixty pounds, at 30 cents a pound, the cost would be only $18.

Check the Cluster

As winter draws near, check the developing winter cluster with an objective eye. Remember, next season and the years to come are all bound up in the genes of the colony queens. If you've the heart, cull ruthlessly. It's not too late to replace queens from swarm-inclined mothers or those that had brood disease or whose workers proved too grumpy or lazy—and some colonies are flat lazy. Any cluster covering less than two full combs both sides (some would say four) should be dequeened and divided up, bees and stores alike, among stronger colonies.

The one year that four of my home colonies turned puny, I combined the two best and requeened them all—the quick way by just introducing the still-sugar-plugged shipping cage right after, I must admit, spending ages finding the old queens. As an experiment, the two remaining small colonies were wintered together in the same hive. I made them separate compartments in the hive with a division board of foam insulation cut bee tight base board to frame top in the brood chamber and in a super above partly filled with honey. They did well over winter and with the fresh queens started the next year with a rush.

Winter Preparations

With the bees medicated, hives weathertight, and stores assured, your colonies are almost ready for winter. In the milder climates, all you need do is install an entrance reducer to keep out mice, and possibly add some top insulation. In snow country, more care is needed.

Top Entrance

Even if snow covers the bottom board and blocks the hive entrance for months, the bees won't suffocate. But they need an exit to make cleansing flights. If your inner cover doesn't have a ventilating port, cut a half-inch notch in the front rim. Shove the telescoping cover forward so the bees can exit easily. Or drill a ⅜" hole through the front of the top hive body midway between one side and the hand hold cut-out. Neither opening will admit worrysome chill but will help to remove moisture-laden air from the hive.

A top pack can be cut from Insulite board or made from a shallow hive body filled with loosely packed hay. Either one placed above the inner cover will act as top insulation, and the hay will provide a moisture absorbant, keeping hive humidity relatively constant over winter, and moderating fluctuations in temperature.

Northern beekeepers once wrapped hives in tarpaper, then drilled a top ventilation and exit hole through. Time-consuming, the practice fell into disfavor when experts found that bees remained healthy if given sufficient stores and the hive interior was dry. After cold starvation wiped out entire apiaries, though, beekeepers fell back on their own expertise and many are insulating hives again. A black (heat-absorbing) cardboard slip-around cover can be purchased. Canadian beekeepers cut foam insulation panels to fit around hives. Either prevents winds from sucking out hive warmth to the point that bees cluster loosely even in −35° blizzard conditions. I've seen hives wrapped in old quilts or horse blankets, and in years past I have packed them in bales of old mulch hay. Check local practice, but if you live in the North, you should consider some winter protection. Many beekeepers believe wind protection, such as shrubs, is enough. But don't airproof the hive, say with a plastic bag. Moist air from bee respiration must escape or the hive will fill with frost.

If snow stays long and deep in your locale, you might consider putting on a top landing board, a wooden lip located below the winter entrance to make it easier for sleep-stiffened bees to land when returning all creaky-kneed from unaccustomed cleansing flights and early spring pollen collection.

WINTER ENTRANCE and LANDING BOARD

INSIDE WINTERING

Before central heat furnaces in basements became common, northern beekeepers wintered single-box colonies in their cellars. The practice of wintering hives inside buildings that maintain even temperature and humidity is returning to the snow belt, particularly in Canada after the mite scares jeopardized annual purchase of package bees from the southern U.S.A.

I winter my half-dozen or so home colonies inside, using a single brood chamber plus a shallow super, as our mountain snows can be counted on to bury hives, and the slush around hive bases can last through April. The house is a 200-year-old unreconstructed colonial with a dirt cellar floor and unmortared stone foundation. I have wood-burning stoves upstairs for heat. Cellar air is humidified by the earth floor and is refreshed every time a wind blows through the old walls. The cellar is dark, and winter temperatures stay between 40° and 50° F—perfect for wintering bees.

Don't try it yourself if you live in a typical North American home with a concrete floor and foundation, and heated basement. Put a hive behind the pool table in the rec room and if the bees don't escape to swarm around the lights, they'll worry all winter and eat out their stores in no time.

In November or early December, depending on the snow, I staple hive bodies and bases together and haul them to the cellar. (Wide hive staples used by migratory beekeepers are sold by many suppliers.)

The hives are placed on pallets that will keep them above any spring water seepage. House mice can be as much a nuisance as field mice, so the entrance reducer stays in, the opening covered by a small bend of window screen that will keep the bees inside when someone turns on the lights to collect a jar of preserves from the pickle chest.

I check colonies every few weeks by rapping on the hive sides. A low hum in response tells me the colony is OK. From time to time I remove the entrance reducer and scoop dead bees from bottom boards, mainly to keep the air flow from being blocked. If a colony's response is too slight, or once or twice a winter in any event, I heat the cellar with a small stove and look into each colony with a strong flashlight, and move full frames of honey near the cluster if they've eaten themselves dry.

Whenever the radio weatherpeople promise several days of unusually warm and sunny weather, I lug each hive up the cellar steps and into the winter air. Entrance reducers come out, the sun warms the hives, and bees take their cleansing flights. A flight every month is not too much, though few winters provide the weather.

Your outside bees will fly, too, when they can. You can don a veil and peek into the upper chamber if the weather is warm. Don't keep the hive open long and don't be tempted to disturb the bees. If there are empty combs at either side of the cluster, remove them and push honey-filled frames toward the cluster. Keep track of stores remaining in the top story of each colony, where the cluster tends to be found in the spring.

ANTICIPATING SPRING

Winter goes slowly for the beekeeper in you. You can while away the time making up accessories—perhaps a box for wild bee tracking. Next year you'll have time to try the involved techniques there wasn't time for this season. You may want to try horizontal-wiring brood frames, hot-waxing foundation onto shallow super frames for comb honey, or studying up to produce section honey. There's plenty of time to mull the catalogs and read the books, send off for new gear, and practice complex manipulations in your mind.

You'll surely want to consider expanding the apiary by dividing your colonies as soon as spring buildup is under way. You'll need a complete hive plus supers ready to go for each division. (Now's the time to try hive bodies with those new corner joints advertised in the bee journals, or maybe a redwood or cypress hive, or even one of the interesting designs from Europe.)

Brood Rearing

Brood rearing will begin when the days start to lengthen, and bees wintered outside, Italians especially, will enter the most dangerous time of year. A spurt in brood food consumption can starve them in a matter of days. So, beginning in late winter or early spring, check your colonies' stores regularly. Even if weather is consistently poor, make at least one check in February—just a peek into the top story will suffice. The cluster will have eaten its way up there and you need only look for capped honey at frame tops. If most frames appear to be empty, give them stored honeycomb, if you have it, or put in a division board feeder and keep it filled with sugar syrup until the dandelions bloom or you know the spring honeyflow has begun in earnest.

For a real emergency, when you find a colony out of food but alive, give them honeycomb or fill empty combs with the thickest syrup you can cook up. Trickle it into the cells through a tin can with little holes punched in the bottom. Put a filled frame on each side of the bees' cluster. You may want to bring the colony into the warmth for intensive care for a few days. Make up cakes of pollen substitute, too, and keep one on the frame tops of all hives needing food until foragers are showing pollen when they return.

Getting Hives Outside

Colonies wintered inside are not as aware of increasing day length, so they don't begin brood rearing as quickly or intensively. (And to be honest with you, I'm just as happy that they don't, and never grow to the 60,000-bee super colonies that require four full hive bodies for roosting space alone, and make record yields, or record swarms.)

I leave my colonies inside until the first pussy willows begin to show buds, and crocuses are pushing up through the rotting snow near the south wall foundation. (If you want to see excitement, take the first spring bloom you can bear to pick to a hive entrance and watch the bees come out and overwhelm it. Now, that's proof that spring has arrived.) Then, out the hives all go, even if I must shovel out their foundations. Checks of stores continue, and feed is provided if necessary.

If hives are kept dry, and cleansing flight opportunities are plentiful, health problems should be minimal for colonies wintered inside or out. Spring is dysentery time, though, so be prepared to dry hives and to feed dry sugar (see Chapter 9 for more information). To avoid more serious problems, treat colonies with Fumidil B against nosema as early as possible. Administer it according to directions in an entrance feeder even if the bees don't really need sugar syrup. Several weeks after the Fumidil, give a course of Tetracyclin as you did in the fall.

Hive Overhaul

When weather is warm enough, do your spring hive overhaul. Check the queen's laying pattern and for brood diseases. Spotty laying, excessive drones, or presence of the less severe brood diseases — especially if the dead brood hasn't been cleaned out — indicate a need for requeening. Reverse dual brood chambers and scrape bottom boards and frames. Cull combs, removing those with more than 10 or 20 percent drone cells. Render the wax and add it to the candle-making supply. Replace culled comb with foundation, and feed 1:1 sugar syrup to fuel the brood and stimulate comb drawing.

A New Year

And now with colonies fed and growing, you are ready for your first full year as an experienced beekeeper. As the days lengthen and the sun brings out the flowers, your colonies will increase rapidly. With most of the brood comb already drawn, all their energy will go into producing young. Weeks earlier than last year, those top inner covers will begin to look crowded, and it will be time to start supering. Then stand back as the honey begins to come in.

Chapter 8

BEES FREE
FOR
THE TAKING

Bees are wild creatures. If hived on your property or mine, they are considered by British common law to be "subjected to man's dominion," and are treated as any other personal or business property. When legally "free to roam at will" as in a swarm, however, they are the property of anyone who captures them. If someone enters your property and walks off with a hive and colony, it is stealing. But if the same individual takes a swarm from your rosebush, the only violation is trespassing. A swarm of bees belongs to the first person to capture it—and that person may as well be you.

Capturing swarms is a time-honored way of increasing the apiary. Indeed, before movable frames came along, it was the only way a beekeeper had to make increase. Hiving swarms remains a valuable beekeeping skill today. You will want to know how to catch the swarms thrown by your own bees. As your beekeeping reputation grows, you'll be asked to rescue the neighbors from swarms that may be viewed as a hazard, especially with the highly publicized Africanized honeybee or killer bee invading from the South. And, you may wish to expand your bee-interest to a real outdoor sport: finding wild bee colonies with an eye to luring a swarm into a home-built trap.

HIVING WILD BEES

My farming Great-Uncle Will called it "linin' bees," and his eyes were so good that he kept at it into his eighties.

"You don't look square at bees once they're flying," he'd say. "Catch them catty-cornered out of the side of your eye, but don't stare or they'll zip right out of your sight and you'll lose them against the sky."

He was teaching me the ancient art and modern sport of tracking bees by determining the flight path or beeline they make from a watering hole or nectar source to their nests. It's a grand weekend diversion for today's beekeepers and, if you attempt baiting swarms, a way to increase your apiary with wild stock.

Back in the forties, after a picnic at the family farm, Uncle Will and I would walk the flat rock pasture creek looking for things that interest country uncles and kids. When we found bees harvesting the meadow flowers or lined up sipping at the brink of a little backwater, we'd "line em."

A water-filled bee would step back, preen and scratch and wiggle for a small eternity. Then, up she would jump, make a climbing turn or two, and head toward home. Bees drink from a wet spot nearest the nest, so we never found more than one colony at one place along the stream, and would know the general direction after only a bee or two took flight. With bees taking off from a berry bush, sourwood tree, or goldenrod patch that teemed with bees, it took some choosing because several colonies would be working the flowers and would fly off in several directions.

Uncle Will would pick a direction in a minute or two, then he'd send me off to the edge of the black oak woods.

Once he was sure I was set right, he'd tie his red bandana to a stick, then poke it into the ground behind the continually arriving and departing bees, and walk backwards until there was a good beeline defined by the two of us and the stick.

I'd look up along the imaginary line every time he'd yell, "She's off!," keeping my eyes wide open but unfocused so as not to limit my range to a certain sector of sky or to a single altitude, and possibly miss the tiny bee.

In time I'd spot one—then another and another and another. I'd call back to my uncle, who'd poke another stick in the soil and join me to confirm my sightings. Then the two of us would walk to the woods, lining up on the sticks in the pasture until the trees swallowed us, then break eye-level twigs along the beeline, always trying to spy out the bee tree which could be anywhere from the woodland edge to the township line.

Lining bees in open country is hard enough. Picking them out from a forest canopy seems impossible at first. Bees fly on a single heading, but change altitude and dodge around obstructions. Spotting the passage of such tiny creatures against a mottled and shifting background of fluttering leaves, waving branches, and glinting sky patches takes patience. You must look for an uncharacteristic straight line—a bee streak—in the varigated natural patterns overhead. It's hard to find the first one, but once you've seen one, you will see them forever. Will had walked his woods since childhood and was able to spot bees better than I ever could, leading us from one open patch to another until the beeline stopped. Then we'd double back toward the last sighting, scanning all intervening trees along the way from ground to top and all around, checking large limbs too. Your eyes have to examine the trees inch by inch, looking for a wispy cloud of entering and departing bees.

It always seemed that I was the one to spot the bees and earn the title of bee finder and full attendant privileges. Forty years later, it seems that the trees I found, and the trees spotted by cousins succeeding me were in the same spots year after year. All of them probably were active and well-known bee trees since Will was a boy himself.

But that didn't spoil the magic. Or the reward, which was a whole great frame of honeycomb cut from the fragrant, brown-stained wood and eaten wax and all—for the bee hunters only . . . well, cutting the comb and enjoying the first sticky serving was.

Not that we felled the trees. Host to wild grape vines six inches through in the trunk, they were too valuable for playing Tarzan of the Apes to cut. We'd get our honey from one of the half-dozen hives lined up behind the strawberry patch, with Uncle Will pulling the comb without smoker or veil and the kids warned far enough away so we couldn't tell whether his claims to be stingproof were fact or not.

Wild Bee Trees

In a generation of beekeeping, I've never cut a wild bee tree and have never seen it done. I do recall Uncle Will telling how they did it in the days of his youth, the 1890s. A man would fell the tree and leave the bees to rest overnight. Then he'd bore small holes into the trunk with a brace and bit. The feel of the wood and borings told him where the hollow began and ended and where the honey and brood comb were. If the nest was in a manageable length of tree – a natural gum some three to six feet long – the section of log containing bees and comb was cut out, capped with planks if need be, and lugged home if the distance was short, or set up with a waterproof roof for repeated harvest in the woods if it wasn't.

To get to the honey, a door was sawed and hand-axed out of the gum. The bee hunters built smoky fires to one side of the tree and fanned smoke into the nest to calm the bees the whole time they were opening the tree and pulling out the honeycomb. Brood comb, containing bee larvae, was usually left and the tree put back together to save the colony for another day. The hunters prided themselves on using no protective gear, and claimed they were never stung. Uncle Will said that there was a ritual associated with getting properly sting-proofed, involving nights spent beside campfires in the woods with a squirrel stew, gallon jugs of corn whiskey, and pipe tobacco that came in fat, black braids to be custom-cut on the spot.

Lining With A Bee Box

Lining a bee tree free-hand takes a concentrated supply of cooperative bees to start with. To track bees working scattered forage, you can make and use a bee box. Any box you can catch a bee in will do, but an elaborate hinged-lid, wooden cigar box is traditional and more fun. Wood cigar boxes are hard to come by these days, but the cardboard moderns will serve.

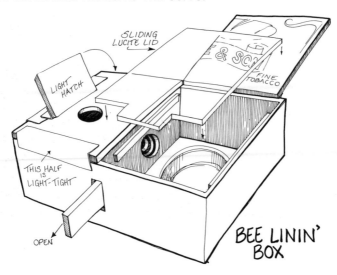

BEE LININ' BOX

Before assembly, the bee lining box's slide and partitions between which it slides are easy to see.

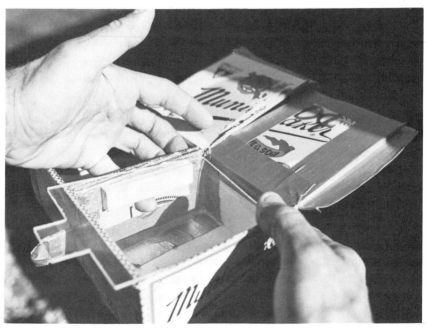

Everything in the lining box is finished but taping down the left side of the lid. You can see my finger poking through the bee portal.

Saw the lid in half along its short dimension, then use pieces from a second box to make a sliding gate between partitions in the center. Drill half-inch bee holes through each partition, and rig a sliding door between them. A length of cigar box cardboard whittled down and inserted between the center partitions through a slot in the side of the bee box makes a good slide if you soak it with paint so it won't wear and frazzle. Use a glossy paint so it will slide readily.

Cut a hole in it that lines up with holes in the partitions when the slide is pulled out, but closes off the trap end when pushed in. Fit the pieces close so the box will be lighttight.

Cut another hole for a light port in the top or end piece of what will be the trap end of the bee box and cover the opening on the inside with glued-on clear plastic (isinglass, stove mica, or thin oilskin was used in the old days). On the outside, fasten one edge of a thin disk with a small screw, so you can open and close the light port at will. Glue down the half lid on the trap end so it seals the box and partition/slide arrangement lighttight.

The other half of the box is the bait end. Cut the front of the box down about an eighth of an inch and glue thin rails inside along the front, sides, and at the back wall so you can slide a piece of clear plastic in to close off the opening whether the lid itself is open or closed. Cut a piece of rigid plastic window glazing (from any country hardware store) so it will slide in and out easily; put a tape flap on the front for easy removal. Glue a jar lid on the bottom of the bait end to hold syrup, and paint the outside of the box and the inside of the bait end whatever color you think best attracts bees. White is supposedly best by scientific bee eye test. Bees I know like light yellow.

Watch Needed

You'll need a watch with a sweep second hand or digital seconds-counter, a little jar of watered honey or thick sugar syrup, plus a good scent—a flowery perfume or the traditional oil of anise which is obtainable at considerable cost from an apothecary. I think that simmering honey is a better bee-attractant than all the perfumes in Araby, so I take along dilute honey, a tin can to simmer it in, and pliers to hold the can with when it's heated over a little propane-fueled camp stove that's good for frying a stream-bred smallmouth bass or brook trout for lunch if I make a full day of the bee hunt, or heating a can of beans if I don't. A section of old comb in the trap end is supposed to be essential, too, but I've never found it mattered one whit. It just melted and made a mess when stored in a hot attic corner over the summer.

Bees For Harvest

If you are out to find a tree to hive a swarm of bees, pick a good day a little before swarming time: late April to mid-June most places—early July 1800 feet up on our New England mountain.

Invite a favorite companion, pack a big lunch and a fishing rod or some good reading to pass the waiting time, and find a nicely wooded spot that's at least two miles from any apiary. No point in spending all day tracking bees through the snags and sloughs of the deep woods just to emerge into a farmer's bee yard.

Honeybees will be buzzing over whatever is most fragrantly in bloom—wild raspberries, white clover, or wild flowers. Open the bait end of your box and tap a bee inside with the flat of your hand. Tap briskly and don't worry about being stung unless you manage to trap and squeeze the bee in your hand or clothing. Close the lid and open the sliding gate and light port in the trap end. The bee will move toward the light; close the gate and she's yours. Repeat until you have a half-dozen or so.

Move out into open country where you can see in all directions. Put some honey or perfume and syrup in the jar lid and insert the plastic cover over the bait end. Close the light port and open the gate to release as many bees as you want to liberate at a time. I try to let out a single bee at first to measure its flying time. It's not easy, as they will all try to boil out.

The bees will move toward the light and buzz at the plastic. Close the gate and the bait end lid. In the dark they will tank up on sugar water. Apply a liberal dose of perfume to the box lid or begin to simmer honey and fill the air with bee lure. After a few minutes or when you hear the bee buzzing to get out, you can open the bait end and release her. Watch the bee as she exits, circles, and flies off. You may get an idea of the beeline immediately.

Time the Flight

Clock the first bee from the time she heads toward home until she returns. They fly at fifteen to twenty-plus miles an hour and spend a couple of minutes offloading at the nest (plus who knows how long dodging branches or crawling along passageways in hollow trees). If your bees don't return in a quarter-hour or so, the tree is over a mile distant. If the wait is over a half-hour, the bees are stretching at the end of their range. Try releasing other bees at another location fifty feet or more away. If they return in four or five minutes, the tree is within 1000 or 1500 yards—within eye range. Seven minutes of flying time equates to about a half-mile, nine or ten minutes to three-quarters. I decide how many miles of timber I'm up to examining branch by branch before I accept a bee's invitation.

Fixing the Beeline

The bee will be followed by her sisters. Step back from the box and watch them come and go until you have established the beeline by lining up your location with the farthest distant object along the line. It's usually a large tree, bush, or hummock.

It may seem that bees will rise, circle once or twice, and then instantly disappear against the sky. You may have better luck spotting them on their incoming trip, and often you can hear the line more easily than see it.

Keep the syrup topped up and the scent lively until you have the beeline. Taking a compass bearing is a good idea to help you get back out of a strange woods. It's cheating if you use it to follow the beeline, though.

From now on you move the box, the scent, and yourself along the beeline in increments, the length depending on topography. You can make longer legs in open country, pretty much have to go from clearing to clearing in the woods, snapping twigs to keep your beeline straight as you travel. When you have a good supply of bees coming and going, and you've pinpointed a distant point along the beeline, begin luring them into the trap end as you did originally. Move along to the far landmark (or beyond so long as you can follow bees flying above), and place the box in a conspicuous place such as a rise in the open or a good clearing in the woods.

Fire up your scent, close the light port in the trap end, open the slide and the lid to expose the plastic cover, and bring the bees out into the bait end. Close the cover to provide the darkness the bees prefer to fill up on sugar or honey. Release them at once or in a series when they are full. They will have to reorient themselves at each move and you will have to reconfirm the beeline and pick out your distant objective each time.

In due course, you'll probably overshoot the bee tree and find the bees heading back the way you came. Then you have to backtrack, looking up as you go. Just remember, the entrance can be anywhere from ground level up—and up, though fifteen feet is a good average height for a nest.

ATTRACTING AND HIVING SWARMS

Finding a bee tree and charting it so you can return is challenge enough for me. I don't hold with cutting bee trees. Too much nest-holed old timber is being culled for firewood or as a timber management practice as it is (already implicated in the loss of the ivory-billed woodpecker in the South and diminution of bluebird populations elsewhere). But you can hive a swarm from your tree, even get started in beekeeping with a wild colony. Very few bee trees are as copious as a Langstroth hive, and feral colonies swarm early and repeatedly. It's been estimated that less than 20 percent of wild swarms find a nest site in sufficient time to put up enough stores to survive their first winter, so hiving one is giving Mother Nature a helping hand. You may also use this technique to bait swarms from your own hives.

Prepare A Hive

Make a bait hive to set up near a thriving colony in the bee tree you've just found. A conventional hive body less frames and foundation is ideal. Cheaper is a sort of giant wren house made of rough planks, chipboard, or plywood. Build a rough box 14″ to 18″ on a side with a sloping top and a hinged side. (Hinging top or bottom would make comb removal difficult.) Be sure the top and side joints are windtight and watertight; tape or caulk them on the outside. Leave a ½″ slit between the bottom and the lower edge of the front

You can hammer up a bait hive in an hour using home carpentry tools. The dimensions don't need to be exact—just build a giant bird house. Note the crossed nails set into the entrance hole. A bee-size hole would be too small to attract the colony; a larger hole left unscreened would admit starlings or squirrels.

panel or drill a 1¼" hole in the bottom of the front panel. Insert and glue nails across the hole to keep out birds and flying squirrels. Old-time bee gum makers would tell you to push a pair of crossed sticks through holes bored in opposite sides of the box (halfway down) to support the hanging comb which is fragile until it's gone through several broods of bees.

Hang the box securely with ropes or use a few easily pulled nails to attach it to a convenient limb some fifteen to twenty feet up in a tree a short distance from but still in sight of the bee tree, so scout bees can find it readily. Bees will happily set up housekeeping in the same neighborhood as the parent colony. Aim the entrance southeast if possible, to catch the morning sun.

Comb Not Needed

Don't be tempted to bait the hive with old comb or foundation. Depending on whom you listen to, it may or may not attract scout bees. But surely it will attract ants or wax moths, which will repel the bees. Check the bait hive as frequently as you can, cleaning out any paper wasps or other small creatures that move in.

Scout bees will appear a few at a time, dodging back and forth in front of the entrance. When you see the steady in-and-out movement of foraging bees indicating that a swarm has arrived, give it a week or two to build enough comb to feel at home. If the nest is not well developed when you open the box, if it doesn't have some comb containing capped brood, the swarming instinct may redevelop and the bees may abscond. I've had that happen with swarms I thought were well and happily housed. Once the bees are settled in, plug the opening one night and haul the hive home.

Transferring the Feral Colony

Set up a conventional hive body complete with ten frames with reinforced foundation. You may need some empty frames tied with string to accept drawn comb from the bait hive (see below). Place the bait hive next to the brood chamber-to-be and open it so the field bees can go to work and get out of your way as you work on the nest.

Before going into the nest, be sure there is a good honeyflow on to preclude robbing. A bait colony comes apart as easily as any other, though the wild strain is likely to be more aggressive than professionally bred bees.

Smoke and lots of it is essential, and be sure to wear your protective clothing. Open the nest slowly and use the hive tool to pry a section of comb from where it is fastened to the top of the box. Check for the foulbroods. If you so much as suspect disease, gas the colony with Resmethrin that night and burn the dead bees, the comb, and the bait hive.

If the brood is healthy, proceed with the transfer. Keep an eye peeled for the queen, in order to preserve her good health if you intend to save her (probably best, to keep the bees from reswarming). Remove her for marking or wing clipping and immediately return her to the colony, or replace her with another queen with better bloodlines (a good idea, but best to wait for a month until the colony is settled in).

Remove the small, outer (honey)combs and rest them against the inside of the brood box, adhering bees and all. Pry out the inner brood combs and insert them into frames, keeping the cells in the original horizontal-vertical orientation.

(I brush off all the bees I can, close up the boxes, and go inside to get away from the milling and understandably upset bees to accomplish the rest of this operation.)

You can fix comb into frames in two ways. First, brush adhering bees onto combs already in the bee box. Then use one of these two methods.

A small section of newly drawn natural comb is inserted into a cut-out in a piece of reinforced foundation. The bees will draw this quickly.

A section of wild comb is inserted between two strings and installed on the frame with a wedge just as you would put on a section of foundation. The bees filled this frame with comb in just a few weeks.

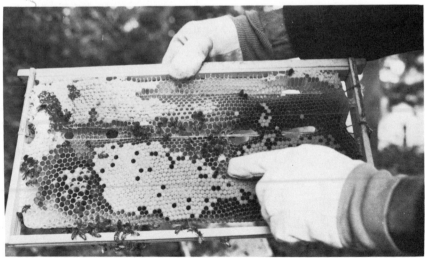

The bees built this section from a couple of sections of wild brood comb from a trap hive. Note the nylon strings still in place. Cotton twine would have been gnawed out and removed.

1. With a sharp knife, cut out wax in the comb's shape from wired foundation already in the frame, slice the comb where crimp wires go, and press it in around the wires and up against the frame top. Be gentle. New comb is fragile, but don't worry about crushing a few cells.

2. Put the comb into empty frames; press it onto the top of the frame by fitting the straight top of each half-oval-shaped comb piece into the kerf left when you removed the splint from the top bar. Then press the splint in on top, nailing it loosely. Slip the flat-topped oval body of the comb into a pair of horizontal loops of cotton twine tied tightly between side pieces. Have the frames ready to go before you remove comb, nails pre-set into frame splints and the string already tied onto the side pieces so you can snub the comb in quickly. Once they get to work, bees will fasten the comb to the frames and chew off the twine, hauling it out to the entrance for you to remove. Put any comb trimmings on the frame tops for recycling.

With your first comb section mounted and placed in the hive, brush the bees from the next section onto the hived comb, and they will stay put. When the bait hive is empty, mount on frames the sections of comb you first put loose in the hive body. Brush the bees left in the bait hive into the new box, fill it with conventional, wired, foundation-filled frames, put on the covers, and sit back to watch the swarm get to work.

Feed these bees for a week at least, especially if there's no strong honeyflow. Don't disturb the colony for two weeks or you could encourage another swarm. Keep an ex-feral colony a good distance from your carefully managed domestic hives, and feed it immediately and again in the fall with AFB-treatment. The following spring, provide a strong Nosema cure. As always, harvest no honey for a month after medicating.

HIVING SWARMS

Would you like to know the greatest thrill I've ever experienced in the bee yard? It wasn't a huge harvest from one colony, but a swarm that rose from a crowded hive to disappear forever over the ridge, with me in hot pursuit so long as I could spot the bees through the treetops.

Chances are, before you see your first swarm, you'll hear it—a low-pitched murmur that grows and swells and builds to fill the air with a gentle but insistent roar. You look up to see this humming, whirling vortex of bees rising and swirling around in a mini-tornado that's twenty feet across and treetop high. A major swarm makes my spine tingle, even if it ends hope for surplus honey that year.

A full super is a full super and the result of manipulation of bees by man. A swarm is nature operating unfettered and free, and I find witnessing one to be considerably more enobling than fingering the $30 to $50 I could get at retail for a super of even the finest section honey. Not that any beekeeper will be spine-tingled by a whole lot of swarms, you understand . . .

Swarming is A. *mellifera*'s only way of perpetuating the species. For reasons covered earlier (and still not fully understood, so never fully predictable), a colony will prepare for swarming by building elongated queen cells around hours-old worker larvae along the bottom of frames. When the new queens are within several days of emerging, the old queen ceases laying and her body shrinks for flight. Young house bees loaf at the bottom of frames while flying-age workers cease foraging and mill around nervously. Large numbers of bees may hang out on the front of the hive.

Then, usually on a good day and usually in mid-morning, about half (usually) of the colony stokes up on honey and swarms (always).

They will form a fairly quiet cloud, mill about for a bit, then will land on any handy support within a stone's throw of the nest and stay there anywhere from a few hours to days. Scouts will look for new quarters, and the swarm will decide on the new location. Then the bees will rise in a tornado again and head off, tail trailing like a Texas twister, toward the new nest.

The main or prime swarm is often followed by one or more secondary or after-swarms with newly emerged virgin queens. A thoroughly swarmed-out colony may be left with only one-tenth of its former strength, but with brood coming on.

Sometimes I divide the brood among hives to strengthen less swarm-prone colonies. Or, if there is enough brood to warrant saving the colony, I give the depleted hive an entrance reducer, and I feed sugar syrup and pollen substitute for three weeks. After the few days needed for a single queen to win out over any of her sisters that emerge, I find and mark her—easy in the depopulated hive—then later replace her with a better queen ordered from the South. Swarming is somewhat a genetic trait and there's little point saving the descendant of a queen proven to be an excessive swarmer.

Saving A Swarm

A gang of 20,000 bees can roost pretty much where it wants to. Most beekeepers are eventually asked to save the neighborhood from such a swarm. If they are your bees, you owe it to the beekeeping community to capture and hive them if you can.

Most non-beekeepers assume that the great, drooping mass of gently humming bees is potentially vicious. That is seldom the case.

They are on a temporary roost, have no nest or brood to protect, and won't sting unless they've been hanging without food and home for several days or weeks.

Some folks may also assume that all of those bees are worth a great deal of cash, which is never the case. Still, I've known people to call a beekeeper and offer to sell a swarm dangling off their lilac bushes.

Unless you are good-hearted or truly want the bees, you should charge whatever you feel your time is worth for solving someone else's imagined problem, plus twenty cents a mile for the driving distance involved. Tell the caller that a swarm of a superior stock might have been worth something two months earlier, but that all these bees will die within six weeks and are good only to build comb for the offspring of a queen of unknown parentage. Besides, you have to provide a $100 hive for them to live in, and the odds of their turning out any surplus honey this year are not very good. Offer the caller some honey the first time the colony produces – and be sure to deliver it for the public relations value to beekeeping in general.

Capturing Swarms

Get to a swarm as quickly as possible. The bees may move at any time. Unless you know how old the swarm is, approach with caution, wearing gloves and head net and with a live smoker or aerosol smoke bomb handy. Some beekeepers take swarms using giant butterfly nets on long poles. Others use ladders to climb around in tree tops. I don't like ladders and tree climbing and I have never tackled a swarm located much above shoulder level. I call the local beekeepers' association when a swarm is beyond my courage level. That group usually has a swarm list and the person on the top of the list is called. You can have your name added to this list if you like.

Most prime swarms led by the source colony's old queen light close to the ground and near the nest. Perhaps this is because the queen has been laying until recently and is too heavy to fly high and far until the new home has been found and the effort becomes essential. Smaller after-swarms led by just-emerged virgin queens will often land higher up.

The bees hang in festoons, loose or tight depending on the temperature, and you can shake a new swarm into anything you can get under it.

The bees prefer a foundation-filled hive. They will usually move right in. Most swarms will fit into a four-frame nuc, or you can use the screen cage your package bees were shipped in. Cut the bottom off a big plastic funnel to fit the opening in the cage or rig your own

1. A medium size swarm droops sleepily from a low shrub. This is a typical height for a swarm's first roost.
2. After filling a hive body with foundation-filled frames, I cut the main branch supporting the swarm. I worked without gloves and with the veil up only after satisfying myself that this was a well-fed and docile swarm.

by stapling several sheets of paper together so you can pour the bees into the container.

Get the hive as close to the cluster as possible before transferring bees into it. The farther the swarm drops, the more upset the bees become. Dropped bees will take flight to rejoin the main cluster, and you will be surrounded by thousands of them, confused and possibly upset.

If the swarm is up high, you may want to support a full-size hive on boxes, a car roof, or a couple of planks set between two stepladders to get closer to the swarm. A good precaution if you have the time is to use a spray bottle filled with sugar water. Soak the outside of the cluster with this water before handling it.

3. I placed the branch with the main body of the swarm in front of the hive. The bees quickly began to move in as I collected small twigs with clumps of bees hanging on them.

4. I caught the queen as she moved over the bees. I found only one here, but there may be several queens in a swarm, usually virgin queens in an afterswarm. Capture the queen only if you have a better queen on hand or on order to give the swarm. Queens are easily injured, and better a queen of unknown qualities than one that is incapacitated.

Try to get the bees off quickly, in one big shake, so the queen will fall immediately. Otherwise, the cluster can split and become confused.

It may want to split anyway, suggesting a multiple-queen afterswarm. If so, you may see several young queens running on the cluster. Capture them separately and make up two nucs if you wish.

If the bees are on a small limb, and the owner concurs, you can hold it very securely, cut it off, trim the ends and hive it immediately, pop it in a box, or wrap it in a sheet.

I carry a standard plastic mesh 100-pound feed sack in the truck and have hauled home a swarm or two in it. Just don't use a plastic trash bag. The bees will quickly suffocate in it.

In-town bees will light on auto bumpers, signposts, or other non-shakeable objects. They must be scooped or brushed off. If the swarm is on a solid object and can't be shaken, support the hive so that the landing board and front of the box protrude right into the swarm. Use a dustpan or a piece of cardboard to scoop some bees into the top and in short order the rest will begin to file into the entrance. If that isn't feasible, rig a boarding plank between bottom board and the swarm. Scoop bees onto the bottom board and into the frames. If need be, gently smoke the rear of the swarm to move it along.

Once the bees have made the group decision to accept the box, you'll see them at the entrance with tails in the air, fanning frantically. Look closely. The final tail segment of each bee is bent down, exposing the Nassanoff gland which releases an attractant pheromone which will bring the flying bees in quickly. You can close the top and wait until all bees are in. At dusk you can move the hive.

Once home with an unhived swarm, you are in for a treat. Keep the swarm cool while you prepare a ten-frame hive. Dump most of the bees on the ground in front of it and make sure that some of them land on the bottom board. Pour some onto the frame tops. You'll hear the bees' humming pick up as they descend into the frames. In short order, they'll turn toward the hive entrance and begin filing into the hive like so many obedient soldiers. Nassanoff glands will be operating overtime. It's one of the truly amazing sights in beekeeping. You can sometimes spot the queen moving along with them, her dozen or so attendants busily grooming her as she goes. If you are Johnny-on-the-spot, you can dab some nailpolish on the queen's mid-section, her thorax, for easy spotting later on.

Put in an entrance reducer and you have a colony ready to work. The hive is a prime candidate for requeening, as the swarm queen is probably a year or more old and of questionable parentage. Here's a chance to send off for one of those hybrid or exotic queens at a summer-season bargain price.

REMOVING BEES
FROM BUILDINGS

Bees in inhabited buildings are a nuisance. They coat the outside of eaves with propolis, and the humidity from bees respiring and evaporating honey causes paint to peel and wood to rot. Removing the bees without damage to colony and building is difficult but possible if you have two months to do it. You must fix fifty or more pounds of hive on a secure platform right alongside the entrance to the in-house nest. In the hive, install either a small queen-right colony, or better, a split of two to four frames of eggs, capped brood, pollen, and honey with adhering bees, but no queen. Fill the rest of the frames with foundation.

You must now find a way to keep all field bees from returning to the building.

Attach a Porter bee escape (how is up to you – the attachment must be bee-tight) or wire screen cone with a half-inch diameter small opening over the entrance of the house colony. Arrange it so the bees can leave, but not return to the colony.

Field bees with nectar or pollen will drift into the box. A queen-right colony will presumably thrive as it is gradually augmented with the house colony's foragers. A queenless colony will raise its own new queen and should establish a vital new colony.

Over a month or six weeks, as it is deprived of foragers, the house colony will dwindle and you'll have all the bees but the old queen and retainers.

Seal in the house colony, old queen and all, for two weeks, then open it and hope your bees will rob out the honey.

Reseal the nest, and assume that wax moths will contaminate the comb so that bees won't return – for a while. This procedure takes a lot of ladder work and attention, and patience on the part of the beekeeper and homeowner. You'll have to tend the new colony in place on the house wall and will probably have to add supers to keep bees from swarming. Then you have to move this hive to your home. I have no idea what to charge for the considerable time and effort involved. And, based on my own experience, I couldn't offer a guarantee that the bees wouldn't be back next season. For a good first-person description of how one experienced beekeeper does it successfully see *The Art and Adventure of Beekeeping* by the Aebis.

Getting Rid of Bees

Our house in town came equipped with a nest that had existed continuously for almost eighty years in the eaves of an attic dormer. A propolis seal extended along the dormer from peak to gutter.

When it came time to refurbish the house, the painters insisted that the bees be done away with before they'd raise a ladder. We didn't have all summer to coax the bees out. The painters' professional exterminator blew powdered insecticide into the entrance and succeeded in killing a few bees, but didn't reduce the colony's flight activity perceptibly.

I drilled holes from the inside of the house to sound for brood and honey, much as in probing a bee tree. Then I pumped two cannisters of Resmethrin into the nest. This killed the colony long enough to get the entrance caulked and the house painted.

But after robber bees attracted by the smell of honey inside the house walls hung around the eaves all summer, a late-season swarm drilled its way in, cleaned house, and repopulated the nest that fall. They are there now and likely forever.

The only way I know to remove bees from buildings and keep them out is to gas the colony, rip the structure open, remove all comb and wood soaked with bee-scent, soak the cavity with a wood preservative containing insecticide and fill it with foam, then seal the whole thing with new building material. Even then a swarm may work out a new nest in the adjoining section of eave or rafter space in years to come.

I've surrendered to our live-in bees, and assume that if they haven't caused structural damage in the last eighty years it isn't likely in the next. We charge the feral colony rent by baiting and hiving its swarms each spring, and we live a peaceful coexistence.

Chapter 9

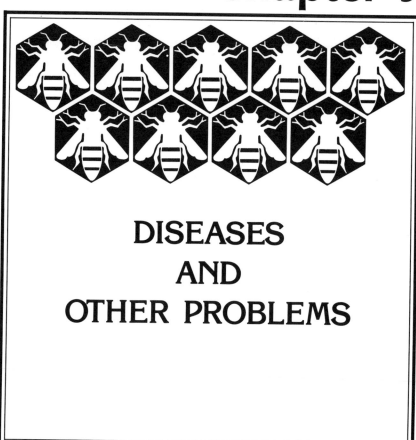

DISEASES
AND
OTHER PROBLEMS

With gentle management, your bees will take care of themselves and provide you with more honey than you need or can give away. But bee pests and diseases do exist and can spread between wild colonies and apiaries. For the good of your own bees and beekeeping in general you must be able to identify the problems, treat them where practical, and call in professional help when needed.

Don't let the following pages discourage you. In a quarter century of beekeeping, I have never seen most of these problems, say nothing of experiencing them. Especially with the aid of modern bee medications, you shouldn't either.

DISEASES OF THE
DEVELOPING YOUNG

The most devastating diseases of Apis mellifera infect the brood, and you must identify and counteract them quickly. Your best bee doctor is a local inspector or other expert. But, remember this address:

Bioenvironmental Bee Laboratory
USDA-SEA, Bld. 476, BARC-East
Beltsville, MD 20705

This is where you will send samples of any mystery diseases of your bees. Cut out a five-inch square of affected brood, wrap it securely but not airtight (so it won't decay and make identification impossible), and send it in a sturdy, crush-proof box to the lab along with your name, address, and a description of symptoms and circumstances that might help with the diagnosis.

American Foulbrood

Bacillus larvae cause the virulent American foulbrood (AFB) which kills **sealed brood**, and Streptococcus pluton is responsible for the less feared, European foulbrood (EFB) which deforms and kills **uncapped** larvae at about four days of age. There are other less severe brood diseases, but presence of either of these may be justification for drastic measures. So destructive is AFB that laws in most jurisdictions give your friendly government bee inspector power to burn infected colonies during his annual inspection.

I was attending a beekeeping workshop at a country living skills seminar some years back when the visiting beekeeper/instructor discovered a festering case of AFB when he opened the hive provided by the seminar promoter for the classes. The teacher, who was also the local bee inspector, dug a pit, waited until nightfall when all the contaminated bees had returned, then he gassed the colony, burned the whole hive, and buried the ashes. This was a bit of overkill, perhaps, by an embarrassed beeman, as the hive bodies, inner cover, telescoping cover, and bottom board (everything but the frames) could have been salvaged with a charring with a blowtorch (or, with more elaborate treatment available at a few bee research stations: immersion for ten minutes in a bath of hot paraffin).

Difficult to Kill Spores

AFB is endemic worldwide, and about 2 percent of all colonies harbor it at any given time. The spores of the AFB organism thoroughly contaminate honey and comb, will infiltrate wood fibers, and live for years through any kind of weather. They will survive freezing and the most thorough scouring with soap and disinfectant, so infected wild bee trees and abandoned "orphan" hives can serve as reservoirs of disease for decades.

Local practice varies. Some authorities burn the whole hive for assured control, while others feel that hive bodies, telescoping cover, and other parts of the hive can be blowtorched, and only bees, frames, and comb from an infected colony should be destroyed.

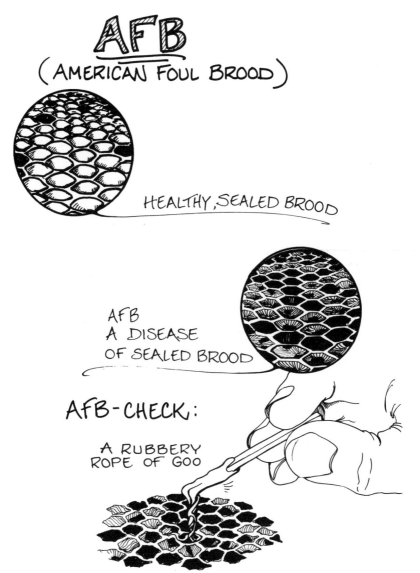

AFB
(AMERICAN FOUL BROOD)

HEALTHY, SEALED BROOD

AFB
A DISEASE
OF SEALED BROOD

AFB-CHECK:

A RUBBERY
ROPE OF GOO

Keeping Control

No colony can survive a severe foulbrood infection, and law or no law, beekeepers, not the government, are responsible for keeping the diseases under control. Any bee, honey, or comb from infected colonies will carry the disease. When your aunt halfway across the continent discards the jar of honeycomb you sent her for her birthday, bees will smell the remaining honey, even a few drops around a closed lid, will burrow into the trash to harvest it, and the disease can be spread.

The foulbroods don't affect adult bees, but swarms or drifting bees from infected colonies will carry the spores, and can pass it to other colonies when foraging or robbing, so foulbrood will spread rapidly within and among apiaries. We must know how to identify it, and be prepared to deal with it when found.

Making a Check

The AFB check is a primary reason to open your brood chambers at least once or twice a year even if you have a thriving colony and no pressing need to check the queen. Go through each frame, checking all brood cells. Healthy uncapped brood will be pearly white and curled at the cell bottom, swimming in royal jelly if very young. Healthy sealed brood will have slightly bulging caps, slightly dimpled at the center, all of them intact and a uniform light honey-gold color. (Of course, you may find capped and uncapped brood, emerging bees and empty cells—all healthy—along with stores on any frame. Or you may find diseased larvae mixed with healthy ones.)

For American foulbrood, look first for scatterings of sunken, discolored, wet, and sick-looking caps, often with irregular holes chewed in them. A badly diseased comb will look and smell sick.

Opening an infected hive can be sickening; foulbrood lives up to its name. Under the sunken cap, diseased larvae will be a uniform, glossy light brown becoming darker as they deteriorate, unlike the varicolored victims of European foulbrood. Poke a match through several suspect caps. If the contents are dark brown and tacky or a lighter brown and slimy and smell of old-fashioned hot horse hoof or brown glue, you likely have AFB.

The bacterium attacks the entire larva in its cocoon after it is capped at six days, slowly melting it to mucus as the larva is consumed and transformed into millions of spores. Pull the stick out slowly. The goo should adhere and string out. If it stretches to a thick, rubbery rope before breaking, it's AFB for sure.

In advanced stages, the liquid dries to a rough, dark brown scale on the lower wall of the cell. Often the mouth of the dead larva will adhere to the upper cell wall at the open end of the cell, leaving a thread of dried tissue that runs back into the cell. Hold the frame at an angle to the light as when checking for new eggs. The dried scales of infections that have run their course will reflect a shiny, mottled light pattern that contrasts with the matte, non-reflecting wax. Unlike the residue of other brood diseases, AFB scales are glued on and the workers can't get them out. If you suspect AFB, but aren't sure, call the bee inspector, or take a frame to a nearby expert. Do it immediately. It isn't fair to other beekeepers (nor is it legal most places) to take time for a by-mail analysis as with less virulent diseases. Be ready to incinerate the colony and treat the rest of your apiary immediately.

European Foulbrood

European foulbrood is harder to diagnose, especially in the early stages, as it is most common in the spring and can be confused with other brood diseases discussed below. It attacks the middle gut of young larvae, causing them to contort into peculiar, twisted shapes before they are capped.

The dead larvae deflate into a sour, dead-fish-smelling, watery paste that won't string out in an elastic rope like AFB. You will see larvae in all stages of the disease. They turn dull white, then yellow, then brown, and then dry into a loosely adhering, rubbery flake at the floor of the cell. EFB isn't all that common in North America, usually goes away of its own accord by summer honey flows, and can be treated more effectively with drugs than AFB.

How to Avoid

Prevention of both foulbroods is possible by administering spring and fall courses of Terramycin made by Pfizer. I treat all my colonies routinely just to keep them free. A packet containing ten grams of medicine (fifty bee-colony doses) in 6.4 ounces of water-soluble powder costs about $5, or a dime a dose (60 cents per colony for two three-dose treatments each year). Terramycin is readily available from bee supply outlets or any veterinarian, feed, or agricultural supply firm. It's a mild and broad-spectrum antibiotic widely used in veterinary medicine. I keep a packet in the refrigerator, handy for a variety of ills of the poultry and four-legged stock as well as bees.

The medicine is unstable in water, so mix the yellow powder with powdered (confectioner's) sugar. It comes in several concentrations, and you should follow manufacturer's directions to achieve a dosage of 200 milligrams of pure medicine per ounce (three level tablespoons) of sugar mix.

Place one ounce (three level tablespoons of mix incorporating 200 milligrams of medication) on a piece of paper atop frames at one corner of the hive. The powder is toxic to brood, so you won't want it to filter down into the nest. The workers will clean it up, then automatically dilute it to a bee-pediatric dose and pass it on to the

EFB
(EUROPEAN FOUL BROOD)

HEALTHY, UNSEALED BROOD

TWISTED LARVAE

DISCOLORED
SHADES OF WHITE, YELLOW, BROWN & BLACK

brood as they are fed. Administer the medication three times, each dose four or five days apart. The antibiotic won't kill the spores, but will protect them from growing and multiplying in the larvae. The antibiotic must not contaminate honey for human consumption, so plan on a month between treatment and harvest. Treat early in the spring, at least a month before a harvestable honeyflow, then again in the late summer or fall after completion of the honey harvest. If you administer the medicine during honeyflow for any reason, don't harvest honey for human consumption for a full four weeks after treatment ceases. Treatment or no, if you find active AFB, destroy the colony immediately. European foulbrood (EFB) infection is thought to be due to a genetic susceptibility in some bee strains. If the EFB isn't too severe, remove and destroy heavily infected comb, treat with Terramycin, and requeen from a different breeder.

Chilled Brood

Chilled brood is common in less vigorous colonies in the spring. Chances are you have a lot more than you know, and just don't spot it before the bees clean it out. A small winter cluster may not be able to cover all its brood during a cold snap, and the outer fringes die from the chill. Dead brood looks dead, without its living gloss and plump grub shape. If brood appears dead in a sort of circle around a patch of good brood, it's likely just chilled. The bees will clean it out.

Chalkbrood

Chalkbrood is caused by a fungus, *Ascosphaera apis*, first observed in California in 1968, and most likely imported from Europe on pollen. Recognized as a severe problem with European black bees since about 1910, it usually appears in the spring, under the moist conditions that favor fungal growth, and attacks both larvae and pupae. The brood dries out, becoming a hard, white mummy, which later in the progress of the disease is covered with black spots, the spores. Often, chalkbrood appears in the same circumferential pattern as chilled brood; the fungus probably attacking cold-killed larvae. Bees will remove the dead larvae, carrying them far from the hive if they can. In typical spring periods of rainy weather, the mummies are left at the hive entrance. You'll see both black and white ones and mixed-color ones, for a quick diagnosis. The fungus usually disappears by early summer's honeyflow, though some colonies may be severely weakened. Some bee strains are resistant and clean it out better than others, Italians being the best. If you suspect chalkbrood, get hives up off the damp ground and into the sun. Requeening with a new and vigorous Italian queen is a good idea.

Sacbrood

Sacbrood is seldom serious, appearing in the spring and killing a few larvae scattered around the nest, but you must be able to distinguish it from AFB. Sacbrood is caused by a virus, and infected comb looks spotty, often with cappings partly chewed away as in the foulbroods. But the larvae don't rot away. They lie on the bottom of the cell, the skin turns leathery and holds the watery contents in a sack, thus the name. As the dead larva dries out, the head turns up like the toe of a wooden shoe, making the scale easy to pick out. If sacbrood persists or affects large numbers of larvae, requeen.

DISEASES OF ADULT BEES

Adult honey bees seldom get sick. The queen excepted, they don't live long enough to incubate many diseases except in the winter cluster. Here is what to look for:

Nosema

In the spring, bees that hang around the hive front, wings at an odd angle, sometimes twitching, may have a mite or paralysis (which see). Most commonly, it's **nosema**, an infection of the bee digestive tract by the unicellular protozoan *Nosema apis*. Nosema is often asymptomatic, and really needs confirmation by microscopic examination of the gut contents. Prevention is the best medicine.

Colonies seldom die from nosema, but can be severely weakened. A *Nosema apis* infection prevents development of the glands that secrete royal jelly in young workers, so diseased bees can't properly feed brood. Infected queens slow down and often stop egg production, and the colony must take time to supersede, losing valuable brood-rearing weeks.

The organism is always present where bees live, but it becomes a problem in the spring when bees are cooped up and unable to fly, or after periods of stress, such as being shipped. An effective control is available, the specific anti-parasitic drug bicyclohexylammonium fumagillin, tradenamed Fumidil B by Abbott Laboratories. It is effective only against the active parasite in the gut of the bee, not against spores, and it must be fed in sugar syrup. The best time to feed is in the fall, when activity of the parasite is at its lowest and when there is least danger of contaminating the honey crop. Package bees are normally treated in the spring to counter travel stress.

Fumidil B is expensive, about $9 for a half-gram bottle sufficient to treat up to six colonies. It comes as a powder and will store indefinitely in a refrigerator.

I measure out a sixth of the bottle's contents, dissolve it in a gallon of 2:1 sugar-water syrup, and feed until each colony has consumed a gallon. I feed it after all the honey is harvested and the colonies are laying in winter stores—about when leaves begin to turn. A dollar and change each fall per colony is good insurance for the backyard beekeeper.

Dysentery

Dark streaks on hive fronts, on comb, and on late winter snow in front of hives in the North are signs of dysentery, which isn't a disease (though bees can have dysentery and Nosema at once). It is caused by excess water in the gut, which is due to damp and wet hives and to granulated or uncured honey. The cure involves time, sunlight, and warmth plus feedings of dry sugar in a hive-top feeder or heavy 2:1 sugar syrup. If the hive front is really messy with streaking, feed heavily.

Paralysis

When paralysis strikes, bees shake and twitch, and can't fly. Often they have enlarged abdomens and may lack body hair from being harassed by healthy workers. The cause is usually a virus. The virus can shorten a bee's productive life by half. If the problem is serious, requeen with another strain of bee from another breeder. No medication is available. Genetic resistance is the only preventative.

PARASITES OF HONEYBEES

It's a small world getting smaller every day, as they say, and along with the social and economic benefits of ever-expanding global trade and travel goes the danger of spreading disorder and disease—bee problems included. We've all read scare stories about the Afro/Brazilian killer bees winging in from South America. These bees (and more about them later) are just the best publicized of several unwelcome immigrants that have come to plague our bees.

In the mid 1980s, the United States and Canadian bee world became alarmed by the threat of foreign bee mites. Mites are tiny members of the class of eight-legged anthropods called *Arachnida*, which includes spiders, ticks, scorpions, and daddy longlegs. Mites (order *Acarina* within the arachnid class) are everywhere, on your houseplants and the dog and in the furniture. The chiggers that cause summer itch are a larval mite. Dry-environment mites live happily in the dust of old houses, causing an allergic reaction in some people, while *Demodex* mites inhabit the follicles of your eyebrows and mine, to no ill effect at all. Several kinds of mites live among bees, the pollen mite *Carpoglyphus lactis* hitchhiking in to feed off stored pollen, and little *Acarapis externus* being a ubiquitous and harmless scavenger on the bee's externals. In declining colonies, mite populations can soar as bees lose vitality and permit contents of the nest to be recycled by wax moths, ants, and mice. Until recently, mites barely deserved notice in healthy North American bee populations.

Acariosis or Acarine Disease (Isle of Wight Disease)

In July 1984 the acarine mite, as it was first called (redundantly), was discovered in six south Texas counties. In flew APHIS (the U.S. Animal and Plant Health Inspection Service), on went federal quarantines, and in a team action like the one mounted against the Mediterranean fruit fly, apiaries were destroyed, states threw up quarantines against bees from other states, the U.S. federal regulators out-quarantined all the states, and Ottawa quarantined the lot.

After fewer than six months of furor, we learned that the suspected hazard, a microscopic arachnid named *Acarapis woodi* Rennie, also termed the tracheal mite, was not a virulent new Pancho Villa Mite invading from Mexico, but had existed all along throughout the prime bee-raising states of Florida and Louisiana as well as Texas, and in at least seven other states. It just hadn't been noticed. Once we begin looking carefully, it probably will show up throughout most of the bee's range. On Feb. 20, 1985, the USDA proposed removing all its hastily imposed restrictions on interstate bee movement due to tracheal mite infestation. And, on April 16, the federal government lifted "all restrictions on interstate shipment of bees and equipment from areas of the country affected by acarine infestation (honeybee tracheal mite)." APHIS concluded that the mite was too widespread to be contained by quarantines, but USDA will continue research to find an effective control. APHIS offers a model quarantine to states wanting to impose one, and most beekeepers will insist that package bees be shipped from apiaries state-certified free from *A. woodi*.

By now most of the dust has settled, with the one positive effect that Canada, long dependent on shipment of package bees from the southern United States each spring, appears to be developing an indigenous bee-rearing program and applying to *Apis mellifera* the same industry that has made Alberta a prime exporter of the solitary alfalfa (lucerne) leafcutter bee, *Megachile rotundata*, which is essential to full pollination of its namesake forage plant. Still, nobody is sure whether acarine disease is the serious threat it was once supposed, indeed, whether it is correctly termed a disease, or just a minor nuisance.

History of the Tracheal Mite

The facts are in perennial dispute, but *A. woodi* may or may not have appeared on the British channel island and county, Isle of Wight, in 1904. Something apparently emanating from there decimated Great Britain's native bees, and whether from the isle or not,

THE TRACHEAL MITE

Acarapis woodi
(MICROSCOPIC VIEW 400X)

SCALPEL

– PIN

BEE MUST BE DISSECTED;
TRACHEA REMOVED
AND EXAMINED
UNDER A MICROSCOPE.

and whether cause of the plague or not, the little mite was eventually found throughout Europe. During the 1920s it was described by a British scientist, John Rennie, who loaned it his name. Italian bees from Buckfast Abbey proved resistant to the disease and were used to repopulate British apiaries.

Today the mite is endemic in Great Britain, where it has been considered essentially harmless by experts since the late 1960s. It was first reported in Mexico in 1980, where few entomologists consider it anything to worry about. Still, some experienced beekeepers continue to consider the little parasite a great danger and take great pains to control it.

Young mites search out newly hatched bees, crawl through the still-soft protective hairs of the thorax, and enter the spiracles or external openings of the bee's forward trachea or breathing tubes — preferring the biggest ones which supply oxygen to the flight muscles. A. woodi takes eighteen to twenty-eight days to complete its life cycle. Newly hatched mites puncture the trachea wall and feed off bee's blood (hemolymph) until old enough to breed and lay eggs. After hatching and molting through several nymph stages (also feeding on bee blood), the young adult mites leave the host and seek out another young bee — worker, drone, or queen. There they move upwind to where the bee is exhaling most strongly and enter the forward trachea.

The mites can't exist for long outside a living bee, so can be transmitted only by bee-to-bee contact. Spread among colonies is not as rapid as it can be with bacterial infections or parasites that can survive independently as adult organisms or spores on combs or in hive debris. The mites spread largely through drifting and robbing bees. Within the colony, only young bees can be infected. Once it reaches the age of five or six days mite-free, the adult has hair that is tough enough so that it is mite-resistant for life. No bee but the queen lives long enough in the harvest season for a serious mite population to build up within its body. If the queen is infested to the point that her pheromone or egg production is affected, she will be superseded.

Like most bee problems, acarine disease can be severe in a weak colony during the high stress period of late winter or early spring, though no one is sure whether the mites cause the weak colony or weakness encourages the mite population. Overwintering bees live for months, permitting the mites to increase, and a severely infested colony can be killed off — again, whether by the mites or other problems or a combination is not yet proven beyond dispute (though a great many British beekeepers who campaign steadily against this mite will dispute that assertion). If you notice debilitated bees outside a hive entrance, wings fluttering or discolored or projecting out at an odd angle, and if inspection shows a distended abdomen, you may have acarine disease (or nosema, which see). For more information, ask for the sheet, *Diagnosis of Acarine Disease*, from the Bioenvironmental Bee Laboratory, Bldg. 476, BARC-East, Beltsville, MD 20705. You need a microscope for positive identification. If you don't have access to one, you can collect fifty lethargic worker bees and deliver them to the local bee inspector, or put them in a secure but not airtight box and send them to Beltsville along with a detailed description of observed symptoms.

Sam gets a close look at the stinger of a bee. A microscope is not a necessity, but is a valuable accessory for a scientifically inclined beekeeper.

Acarine Disease Controls

The Frow treatment used in Europe is dangerous to both you and your bees. A mixture of gasoline and nitrobenzene, it may kill your bees and just might blow up on you. I don't think I'd like to have a drop of it touch my skin, and rather than use the Frow treatment, would let a badly infested colony die out, and repopulate with package bees next year. The mites won't live long without a living host.

The summer-season acarine treatment is less hazardous to everyone's health. Pick a warm but not hot evening and block the hive entrance. You remove the inner and outer cover, then put an empty super over the hive and suspend in it under an airtight cover a smoldering strip of Folbex Forte. This is the trade name for cloth impregnated with *chlorobenzilate*, a specific miticide. The bees will circulate the smoke as they fan air through the hive. One strip per brood chamber is recommended. Give two treatments of an hour apiece a week apart.

At this writing, the therapeutic materials are not commonly sold in North America, though you may be able to get a just-in-case supply from overseas. The British firm Robert Lee (bee supplies) Ltd. sells Frow mix and Folbex strips. Other miticides used by researchers have included methyl salicylate, methanol, and menthol. None is without its hazards to bees and beekeepers.

Probably the best long-term solution will be to breed mite resistance into bees, but no one is sure what is needed or whether it is worth the trouble. As with most bee problems, the best cure seems to be prevention, maintaining strong colonies with a good queen in dry quarters.

Varroasis

Varroa jacobsoni is another bee mite, this one an ectoparasite that lives on the outside of the host. It is a natural parasite of the eastern honeybee, *Apis cerana*, which transferred to our friend *A. mellifera* a while back when beekeepers took some colonies visiting Asian Russia and points east. *Varroa* now exists most everywhere but in North America, Australia, New Zealand, and Great Britain, but its spread to the English-speaking world is almost certain.

I hope that you never see *Varroa*, but don't mistake the harmless little flightless fly, *Braula coeca*, or bee louse for the mite. *Braula* is an occasional freeloader in bee colonies, often found riding on the thorax, or middle body segment, of bees—seldom on the abdomen where you'll find *Varroa*. *Braula* is a bee's eye-sized bug with distinct head and body segments and six long, springy legs; it jumps when

VISIBLE PARASITES

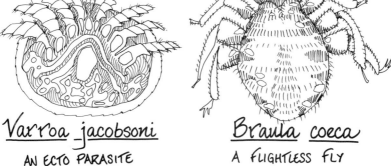

the size of a Bee's eye...

Varroa jacobsoni
AN ECTO PARASITE

Braula coeca
A FLIGHTLESS FLY

disturbed. *Varroa* looks like a miniature, $\frac{1}{16}$ inch wide, oval crab. It's a slow-crawling, eight-legged creature, a medium red-brown color, a little smaller and a lot lower-to-the-bee than *Braula*.

Varroa females prefer to lay eggs in drone cells. The young mites hatch, feed on developing larva, and breed inside the capped cell. The small, pallid males die and the reddish-brown females emerge to feed on adult bees and perhaps catch a ride to a new hive on a drifting bee. Curiously, unless infestation is severe, bee larvae parasitized by the mites emerge in fine form. In serious infestations, adult bees are said to exhibit malformations of legs, rear body segments, and wings. The adult females obtain bee blood by puncturing soft tissue between the under-abdominal scales of their adult bee hosts. They live from sixty days in summer to eight months in the winter cluster.

Minor *Varroa* infestations are hard to detect. In Europe, where *Varroa* is well established, beekeepers use winter inserts. Each fall a sheet of paper is placed under a coarse (3mm or about ⅛″) screen that's held by a frame just a fraction of an inch above the bottom board. Dead mites will fall through, bees can't clean them off, and the beekeeper can check at will. If you do find *Varroa*, collect the mites plus any infested bees you can locate, and send them to Beltsville special delivery.

To date no effective treatment is known. The mite is reportedly most dangerous in cool climates such as our own New England, so I for one will stay on the alert.

Varroa Mites on a pupating bee

inside the cell

Mites on Adult bees:

Varroa on the abdomen

Braula on the thorax

Bee Louse

The bee louse, *Braula coeca* Nitzch, is discussed above along with the Varroa mite. A flightless fly, the adults hitch rides on bees' thoraxes and reportedly tend to gang up on the queen, but apparently do no harm other than to take a little of her food as she eats. Eggs are laid in the comb and the tiny larvae burrow around under the cappings. Their tunnels could be mistaken for the lesser wax moth and will detract from the appearance of comb honey but do no harm otherwise.

Braula is uncommon in North America, but the old books say to smoke with tobacco leaf. Since nicotine can kill bees too, I'd hold off treatment, and send a sample to Beltsville for the most current information if infestation is severe.

PESTS OF HONEYBEES

Ants and termites pose a serious problem to bees, especially in mild climates. Ants so small the bees scarcely notice them will bivouac in the telescoping top or constantly stream in and out through cracks in the bottom board, burgling stores. A foraging army of an aggressive ant species will invade, often chewing their own entrance through the bottom board, to consume wax and honey or kill and carry off bees and brood. Termites will cheerfully gnaw the hives bodies to wooden sponge supported only by a shell of paint. To avoid this damage, place hives on stands with the feet

Carpenter ants like a high, dry place, like the top of this inner cover, to raise their young in the spring. I brushed them out. Later, when the new colony was strong enough to retain its warmth in our cool climate, I opened the cutout on the inner cover so the bees could keep the ants at bay.

in lagoons of oil (that you must keep clear of debris and replenish after rains). Or protect the hives with gummy "tangle-foot" type barriers that must be kept fresh and sticky. Approved insecticides can be used to poison subterranean nests, but anything that will poison ants or termites will kill bees, too. Use with care and bury the chemicals deep if they are used near the apiary. Don't use them at all if your hives are anywhere near your well or a water supply used by any other life form that's meaningful—and what isn't?

Bears

Bears can be a terror in the north country. An electrified garrison fence around the apiary is the only effective barrier I know. Find someone local who keeps hogs successfully, and take his advice on bear-proofing your bees.

Birds

Birds, such as jays or purple martins, will catch bees on the wing, but seldom in sufficient numbers to matter. A large flycatcher or jay may set up shop on a branch above a hive and eat a colony out. I keep a sweet little .410 shotgun for such marauders. Check the legality of such action in your state before following suit.

Bugs and Such

Assorted nocturnal wet creepies, including earwigs, centipedes, **sowbugs** (which aren't bugs at all, but those little grey crustaceans that roll up in a ball when disturbed and are also called pill bugs or wood lice), and other woodland scavengers will live in and under a too-wet bottom board. Get the entire hive up off the ground and in the sun. A cement block base will permit air to circulate and keep the baseboard dry.

Assorted nocturnal dry creepies such as scorpions, horned toads, and sidewinders will seek daytime cool and shade by digging in under a beehive in some areas. Let them sleep in peace.

Skunks

Skunks visit bees at night, scratch at the front of the hives, and lap up the bees as they come out to investigate. A skunk will happily make its living off your bees all summer long. Colony populations will fall unexplainedly, and the bees that remain will become testy.

Look for claw scratches on the hive front, matted grass or tracks in soft soil in front of the hive, and dark animal droppings containing empty bee carapaces. A two-foot high hive stand will keep them honest. They'd have to stand on hind legs to get at the bees, exposing a soft underbelly to stings.

Poisoning skunks is effective but best done under authority and control of the local fish and game authority or your Extension Agent. Leghold traps are a nasty way to trap skunks. Live trapping with a meat-baited Havahart type trap will work, and I've done it. You approach the trapped skunk slowly at night, keeping a flashlight shining in its eyes. Cover the cage with a dark cloth and carry the animal off. Open the trap in a remote locale, and the skunk will run out happily. As with bees, just don't move fast or unexpectedly in the skunk's presence and you won't get spritzed. It works, honest.

I admit, I've had some practice in skunkery. I kept an orphaned skunk all one summer but didn't de-skunk him so he could go wild when grown, which he did. We learned to give him leeway when his tail went up over his back and never got sprayed—except the time that my son Sam accidentally spilled a harvest of fresh hen eggs on his head.

North American **toads and frogs** have been known to eat one bee, but only one. Tropical species with apparent immunity to stings will squat horribly in front of a hive and use their long, sticky rubberband tongues to snap up bee after bee. Putting the entrance in upper hive bodies, or the hive on a tall base, will keep them out of range.

Mice and Voles

Mice and voles will overwinter in occupied hives, building nests in the outer combs away from the winter cluster. Hardware cloth barriers or entrance reducers installed in the fall will usually keep them out. In some high mouse-population years, they may chew their way in. If you are in a mousy part of the country, a little wedge of D-Con mouse bait placed beneath the hive base will help. Rats and mice can ruin stored comb and gnaw up fragrant, honey-smelling woodenware. A few frames can be kept in a strong chest or closet. Normal farm rodent controls are in order for any larger scale storage.

Moths

The **wax moth**, *Galleria mellonella L.* is a fall-season nuisance throughout North America and is a serious threat to comb in heated storage or in frost-free areas where the moth has several generations each year. The adult is a ¾", bean-shaped, grey-brown miller moth that likes to roost on the sides of hives and, when disturbed, will scuttle off before flying. It is part of nature's marvelous recycling plan. In late summer when bee activity is winding down, female moths lay eggs near soon-to-be vacated bumblebee and other native bee nests, and on the outside of honeybee boxes. Tiny larvae tunnel through the thinnest cracks to burrow through the comb, feeding on hive detritus. When grown, they travel very fast, looking for all the world like miniature high speed streamlined trains, speed being their prime defense against bees. They bind up gnawed out comb with mats of web and spin cocoons in the gruesome mess that's left.

Strong bee colonies control the wax worms easily, but they ruin undefended or stored comb. You can imagine what a single larva could do to a frame of comb honey you send as a gift, and your friend stores the valued present in the kitchen cabinet for a time. When it comes time to open up the comb for breakfast toast . . . Ech! More than one southern beekeeper has constructed a refrigerated room for comb storage (and others have resorted to selling the wiggly moth larvae as bream bait).

EDB, ethylene dibromide, has been an approved fumigant, but is now acknowledged to be a hazardous chemical, and its use can't be recommended.

The only approved fumigant for comb containing honey for human consumption is carbon dioxide gas that suffocates the moth eggs and larvae. You must keep the comb in an airtight chamber containing a 98 percent concentration of CO_2 for four hours at 100° F and a relative humidity of 50 percent. That's a bit much of an undertaking for a hobby beekeeper.

Like all lepidoptera larvae, the wax moth is susceptible to the garden spray BT (Thuricide and Dipel are trade names), which contains spores of *Bacillus thuringiensis*, a pathogen of caterpillars that is harmless to bees or humans. The spray is noxious smelling and is unsuitable for applying to comb honey, though the powdered version can be dusted on empty comb and in woodenware.

The young moth larvae begin life by drilling through the comb's center rib, so extracting foundation treated with BT spores can be effective, but is as yet hard to find commercially. The best use would be in foundation for comb honey, but, harmless though it may be, no one wants to ingest the stuff even if it were legal. A double bind.

Small-scale beekeepers can destroy wax moth eggs and larvae by keeping comb honey in the deep freeze for several days. Wrap it well in foil or plastic to keep freezer smell from tainting the honey and be sure it reaches 0° F.

Protecting Comb

You can fumigate and store drawn but empty comb by storing it in plastic sacks containing moth crystals — paradichlorobenzene (PDB). Put about a tablespoon of crystals in a paper bag. (It can corrode metal and melt some plastics on contact.) Pin the bag so that the crystals don't touch wood inside a frame-filled super that you tie up airtight in a plastic trash bag, which won't be hurt by the fumes. The PDB gas will kill the larvae as they hatch and will repel any adults in an egg-laying mood, but will not kill the eggs. It is toxic, and will contaminate cappings, so never use it to fumigate comb honey. Air treated comb for at least twenty-four hours before using it.

There are other nuisance moths — the lesser wax moth is common in some parts of the Pacific Northwest — that will bother comb. Treatment against the greater wax moth will control them all.

Wasps

Wasps, in particular a new and more aggressive North American variant of the little bright yellow-banded vespid wasps we call **yellow jackets**, that buzz your watermelon during late summer picnics, can wipe out entire bee colonies. In the fall, yellow jacket populations increase to rear males and the queens which, after mating, will hibernate over winter. Larvae are fed on masticated insects, and bees carrying loads are easy prey. The wasps will kill a bee in the air, ride it to the ground, then remove its head and thorax and fly off with the abdomen. Presence of bee carcasses without abdomens in front of a hive suggests wasp predation. Yellow jackets from a nest within 200 feet of a bee hive will kill the guard bees, then invade and decimate the colony. Try to spot an attack and trace the wasp to its nest, a small hole in the ground in heavy brush or other cover. The nest is an underground version of the familiar gray paper wasp nest found hanging in bushes and under eaves.

At night, pour in enough liquid insecticide to fill the nest. I make up a gallon of an approved insecticide and pour it in through a large funnel, then put a large, flat rock on the hole. Any contact-type bug killer that will destroy ants or termites will kill wasps if you can catch and keep them underground.

KILLER BEES

On the morning of July 26, 1985, the wire services reported that a colony of the Africanized honeybee (AHB) had been discovered in Lost Hills, Kern County, in the San Joaquin Valley of central California. The killer bees, subject of lurid journalism and "B" movie plots for a generation, had arrived in North America a half-decade earlier than predicted.

On the CBS Evening News that night, Dan Rather and company showed a videotape of the just-gassed colony being dug up, featured a local citizen describing how a rabbit, a kit fox, and a raven were supposedly stung to death by the swarm, and stated with authority that the AHB chased away our own gentle honeybees, but wouldn't pollinate farm crops, so was sure to be disastrous for agriculture. And more swarms were at large!

For years we'd been exposed to similar half-truths about this hybrid bee as it worked its way north, swarm by swarm, from South America.

Back in 1956, Brazilian researchers imported some of the African strain of honeybee, *Apis mellifera* adansonii, (*A. m.* scutellata in some classifications) for hybridization studies. In 1957, despite careful security measures, and under what some consider suspicious circumstances, twenty-six colonies in Sau Paulo state were liberated and began interbreeding with the native strain, western honeybees that came to the Americas with the first European settlers. Swarms of the hybrid bee produced by the African/European mix radiated out from southeast Brazil at 100 to 300 miles a year. By 1982 they were across the isthmus and into Costa Rica heading toward

Mexico, predicted to hit Brownsville, at the southeast tip of Texas, some time between 1988 and 1990.

Arrived by Accident

The sudden appearance of African bees in 1985 was an accident of international commerce. They most probably hitchhiked in on oil field equipment brought up from South America. California officials killed the parent colony, but empty queen cells suggested that four swarms had been thrown before it was discovered. An early plan to mount an aerial spray campaign to kill every bee in the San Joaquin Valley was abandoned in favor of a quarantine of 400 square miles and hive-by-hive examination and by-hand extermination of all wild colonies in a fifty-square mile area by a twenty-hand SWAT team. Still, the press continued to foster suspicion that not all the killer bees had been found – a harbinger of popular reaction to swarms that would be arriving in unstoppable numbers in the near future.

No Threat To Humans

As federal and California officials and bee experts nationwide took great pains to point out, the AHB is not a threat to humans or pets and livestock, though its impact on agriculture is an open question. This strain of *Apis mellifera* (the same species and descended from the same rootstock as our own sweet-tempered bees) evolved in the sub-Saharan region of central Africa. As we all know from the tragic famines there, this is a harsh environment subject to periodic drought. Like food for humans, nectar and pollen can be hard to come by. Living proof of the old adage "when the going gets tough, the tough get going," the African bees are small and resiliant, willing to exploit a wide variety of food and water sources and easily able to out-forage their relatives that developed in the easy living of the European tropics.

A. m. adansonii also developed the habit of moving frequently in search of food and water. At the slightest provocation, they will abandon a nest brood and fly off to construct a replacement in a more favorable locale. Proper quarters aren't always at hand in the semi-desert, so bees will move into burrows, evicting and sometimes stinging fatally the small-animal tenants, or build comb in the open, and then defend the exposed nest in an aggressive manner.

This protective behavior may also be a reaction to centuries of human exploitation. Wild nests have long been hunted and burned out for their wax. Today, Africa is the major source of beeswax imported to North America, largely by the cosmetics industry.

Super Bee

The aggressive African drones originally released in Brazil proved to be superior breeders, and the hybrids produced by the cross between the AHB and indigenous bees is a true super bee. According to some researchers, queens produce 3,000 or more eggs a day, compared to the western bee's day rate of 1,000 and up. An AHB worker reportedly forages herself to death in only two weeks, compared to about six weeks for a European strain.

Stories of children and livestock being killed from unprovoked attacks have been wildly exaggerated, but have a basis in fact. That first North American swarm may indeed have killed a small kit fox when the colony took over its den. Unaccustomed to so aggressive a bee, the fox would have defended its home, and lost the battle.

Reliable studies have found that Africanized bees are prone to sting six to eight times to the European strain's one and will fly out to protect their nest when calmer strains doze sleepily. Honey production is reportedly tremendous, but harvesting it can be harrowing. When a hive is opened, the guard bees erupt from the hive in furious attack while younger nurse bees run choatically on the combs. These characteristics have been largely bred out of our strains.

Small Beekeepers Affected

Statistics from Argentina indicate that up to 80 percent of backyard beekeepers have been driven from the hobby, while commercial beekeeping has fallen by 20 percent in areas of the country colonized by the AHB. First-hand reports from visiting North American beekeepers confirm that Africanized bees are too aggressive to be kept by most hobbyists or to be housed near populated areas. Guard bees will fly out to protect an area in front of the hive, not up to twenty feet as our own bees might, but up to 200 feet. Once alerted, the colony will chase an interloper for up to a half-mile, not the fifty or hundred feet that any beekeeper has been pursued by the occasional single "mad bee" that takes a dislike to him.

If disturbed by human activity, the colony will abscond to fly up to twenty miles away. That's an impossible trait if the bee is to be kept for honey production or pollinating service. Then a favorite new home may be a hive of Western honeybees, which is simply outgunned and evicted by the little hybrids much as strong colonies will rob out and kill the weaker in periods of nectar dearth.

Hard to Identify

Only an expert can differentiate this bee from another strain. It is a matter of comparing patterns of veins in wings, size of the fore-wing, and nature of the underbelly wax glands. There's as yet no quick and easy identification technique.

Contrary to some published reports, an AHB sting is no worse than any other and they don't sting on forage any more than an Italian. The only obvious difference is in behavior around their own nest where they are aggressive, unpredictable, and extremely defen-sive. It seems that the bees' unpleasant personality retains genetic dominance despite thirty years of inbreeding with gentler bee strains, so predictions that a few more years' natural interbreeding will sweeten them are surely wishful thinking. For now, we're stuck with the AHB, unpleasant as it may be.

Economic Impact

The USDA is studying the AHB's effect on the agricultural econ-omy in areas of Argentina where the climate is similar to ours. More data will be in before the bees invade North America in large num-bers. A preliminary report predicts the U.S. bee industry alone could lose $26 to $58 million a year if the AHB affects us as it has our neighbors to the south.

Even more significant economically, much of our agricultural production is directly dependent on honeybee pollination, and much of that on the services of migratory beekeepers who truck their colonies from field to field over the growing season.

Press reports to the contrary, the AHB is perfectly willing to feed from and pollinate flowers of farm crops. But their easy absconding habit and quickness to anger makes the strain unsuitable for migra-tory pollination service. Agribusiness will surely find a way to keep the land productive, but dislocations may be created and farming techniques may be affected, which could be costly. For example, the California almond industry alone is totally dependent for polli-nation on migratory honeybees and supplies a third of the world's almonds, worth over $80 million a year. In July, 1985, Dr. Marshall Levin, director of the Carl Hayden Bee Lab in Tucson, Arizona, hypothesized that a doubling of hives might be needed to pollinate almonds successfully with the AHB, raising the pollination fees for a 100-acre grove from $2,800 to $5,600 per year. And, that's if bee-keepers continue charging today's $25 to $30 per hive per season, unlikely if they have to replace frequently absconding AHB colonies or laboriously keep their European stock AHB-free. Costs of bee-pollination crops in the AHB era are likely to rise, and we'll all pay the difference one way or another.

A Cold-proof Bee?

Some researchers are convinced that the AHB is not frostproof and never evolved a winter clustering habit in the warmth of its native Africa, so won't survive in parts of the northern United States and Canada where winters go below 15° F or where there are fewer than 240 frost-free days a year. There is little doubt among the experts that all wild and naturally bred colonies south of a line extending roughly from North Carolina, dipping down to North Texas, then across the continent to mid-California and on up the Pacific Coast to the Canadian Northwest will be thoroughly Africanized by the turn of the century and perhaps earlier. Swarms will surely venture north to establish temporary colonies, but no one knows how far north the cold-kill line will extend. The bees may summer on the East Coast as far north as New York City, and some will overwinter successfully for limited periods.

Other researchers find that A. m. adansonii has adapted to a certain amount of cold, as loosely clustering colonies have been found in the chilly mountain altitudes of South Africa where night temperatures dip below freezing for six months a year and snow lasts for a week or more at a time. Whether this potential exists or will emerge in the Brazilian hybrids is not known. For now, the beekeeper in me can be thankful for the weeks of below zero cold we endure each winter here in New England.

Immediate Implications

Over 90 percent of our package bees and queens are raised in southern latitudes that will be Africanized for sure. The package bee and queen-rearing industry has yet to face the AHB threat directly, but leaders are working on it. No one seriously believes that a selective eradication program as carried out in mid-July 1985 in the San Joaquin Valley can be sustained continent-wide. Within a few years, any queen in the AHB zone permitted to breed naturally will surely be inseminated by AHB drones.

One breeder I know is considering several options such as a move north, a move to an offshore island, or production-line artificial insemination. The breeders will find a way to supply good bees, but the method and price have yet to be proven in the marketplace. The cost of package bees is sure to skyrocket, along with the value of home-raised honey. I'd suspect that artificial insemination will become more common, and the value of a proven, inseminated queen will be many times the cost of today's naturally bred queens.

Isolated Islands

Queen-raising on isolated islands where the occasional accidentally introduced alien insect could be selectively eradicated has already shown promise for the Hawaii-based Kona Queen Company, started by two U.S. breeders, partly in anticipation of the arrival of the AHB. They experienced initial interference from brown bee drones from native colonies, a problem reportedly solved by studious isolation of mating yards.

We may be ordering queens from other islands too, though recently stiffened American and Canadian bee and bee product import restrictions will make foreign queens hard to come by until a workable inspection or quarantine procedure is established. The small indigenous northern American and Canadian queen-rearing industry will continue to grow and the south-to-north flow of queens may be reversed over time.

My Answer

For my own part, I plan to become even more resolutely independent as a beekeeper rather than falling back on package bees as in the past. I've already put together a set of cell cups and a grafting tool and will try raising my own queens from the best colony every year. I may read up on artificial insemination and try that in time. Like you, if you are interested, I'll be studying up on queen-raising over the coming winters. I have begun marking queens with the little German-made numbered tags sold by some suppliers, so as to be able to identify queens closely and replace them before they are naturally superseded, possibly by an AHB-bred queen. This will mean more frequent hive inspections and more carefully honed queen-spotting skills and probably more intensive brood manipulation schemes.

In sum, the impact of the AHB on you and me as backyard beekeepers will be what we make it. If we want, we can keep our colonies AHB-free with more effective queen and swarm management, surely using practices yet to be developed in face of problems yet to be encountered. There will be many questions. What do we do when an AHB swarm appears one day to invade a colony of sweet-tempered Italians and chase you from your own apiary? If you gas the hive, you will lose the frames of growing Italian brood and contaminate stored pollen and honey. I suppose you could vacuum out the AHB colony at night; that might require a new design engine-powered tool, a reverse-geared mechanical bee blower perhaps. Could you anesthetize the AHB swarm with CO_2 and replace the queen, and if so, how much do you apply for how long? Perhaps another bee tranquilizer will be needed. Must we develop night-handling techniques to isolate, trap, and replace an AHB queen in a colony of bees that doesn't respond well to smoke and that runs on the comb? And what special queen-introduction techniques are needed to civilize an AHB-tainted colony?

The unanswered questions are many, and, given the inevitability of the AHB invasion, comprise a challenging opportunity for creative beekeeping. If you come up with the management practice that solves all our AHB problems, let me know. Or better yet, let us all know and publish your ideas in the bee journals.

ROBBING

Field bees, Italians in particular, are continually probing the defenses of alien hives. The less nectar available on forage, the more they go foraging for the goods of other colonies. When a bee manages to fill up on someone else's honey, exposed nectar, hive scrapings left carelessly around an apiary, or on syrup from an accessible entrance feeder, she recruits her sisters and they go on the warpath. Robbing excites bees and can excite an entire apiary. Robbers first become obvious as a cloud of bees in front of the hive. They don't act like purposeful foragers, or fly the zing-it-to-you beeline of a defender, but buzz loudly, swirling around or darting in rapid, erratic patterns, often with their legs dangling unnaturally.

Don't mistake for robbers these two other clouds of bees:

1. House bees newly graduated to foragers, on their first flights. They fly around randomly in front of the nest, flying up and down a lot, with a gently fluffy soft of buzz as they orient themselves to landmarks.

2. Bees kept from landing by the wind. They aren't very wind tolerant at landing speed, are grounded by a wind of twenty-five miles per hour, and inhibited by velocities of fifteen miles an hour. Here on our mountain, there is often a cloud of foragers in front of hives, fighting a breeze that we barely notice.

With study you may see bees entering a hive in an unnatural, sneaky manner. They approach one at a time from the side, sidle past the guards at the corners of the entry or squeeze through cracks between supers. When a single sly robber is discovered, she is usually just hassled out of the hive by the workers. You'll see the alien bee rest in the grass in front of the landing board, adjust her ruffled wings and smooth messed-up body hairs. She will wiggle and grouse a bit, then fly home none the worse for her transgression.

This progressive robbing takes place all the time, and can't be controlled.

If serious mob-robbing proves successful and waves of robbers return with more reinforcements, you can find yourself engulfed in a cloud of excited bees in short order. Hive bees and invading robbers will grapple, fighting to the death at the hive entrance.

Robbing is the only unattractive bee behavior I know. It's nastier somehow than stinging, which is an honest protective response. If not halted, robbing bees can invade a colony, kill the guards, then murder the inhabitants and strip the colony of its stores. It is a way to import disease to your apiary even if the colony survives. If a hive is attacked, close it quickly, stuff grass in the entry so guard bees can defend it more easily, and get out your garden sprinkler. Set it on the top of the hive and run at a fine spray to simulate heavy rain. This tip (from the excellent book, *Practical Beekeeping in New Zealand*) is the only practical way I've ever heard to stop robbing once it has started.

PESTICIDES

So-called "organic" pesticides that deter or kill target pests without harming the rest of the environment are coming into increasing favor in an ecology-conscious world. But broad-spectrum insecticides are still too common in a society that has come to expect picture-perfect lawns and blemish-free apples. You must be on the alert for dusting or spraying of any toxin that poses a serious threat to your bees. Don't be concerned about a neighbor dusting the garden beans with rotenone or putting a systemic insecticide around the roses; it's large-scale applications to bee forage plants in bloom that can harm your colonies.

Toxins Not in Honey

Fortunately, you needn't be concerned about insecticides contaminating your honey. There are very few instances of poisons being found in the honey itself—even from heavily sprayed citrus- or cotton-growing areas in the past DDT era. Bees are delicate creatures, and usually die before getting back to the nest. Those that do make it back are usually affected sufficiently by the toxin that their erratic behavior causes guard bees to eject them before poisoned nectar is added to the honeycomb. It is the adult bees themselves that are at greatest hazard and entire apiaries have been lost, or colony populations reduced to nonviable numbers by insecticide applications.

Foraging bees can be killed by nearly any freshly applied insect poison spray. Soil fumigants are breathed in. Contact-type toxins enter their soft bodies through pores. Bees ingest gut poisons while taking up nectar.

Dusts can be even more dangerous, as the pure toxin can be taken back to the hive on the bee's body hair or in pollen from which it can be transmitted to brood, nurse bees, and the queen. Most lethal are the modern time-released insecticides which will meter out poison to the colony over an extended time.

The large bee reference books list agricultural insecticides that are toxic to bees, if you are interested. This information is of limited value to the novice beekeeper with little knowledge of local agriculture. The best source of practical pesticide information is your local beekeepers' association; many members will have sickening bee kill stories to tell. Alternatively, the county agent will know when local farmers, road crews, or timber management firms apply bug killers to large acreages.

Protecting Colonies

To protect your bees, find out:

- **When the poisons are to be put on.**
- **To which flowering plants they are being applied.**
- **The duration of the poison's toxicity.**

So long as the toxin is potentially hazardous, and that's as long as an active toxin is on a fresh-flowering forage plant, keep your bees at home. Close the entrance of each hive with a fine screen mesh at night when all bees are home. Don't use an entrance reducer with the opening screened if weather is at all warm, as the colony may be unable to ventilate the nest while the entire foraging force is cooped up on the comb. Indeed, if weather is extremely warm and colony a strong one, you should put a screen cover on top of the hive and block up the telescoping cover enough to let air escape.

If your hives are located in an area scheduled for dusting or spraying (as in an out-apiary located in a field or orchard) and they can't be removed, you should plan to cover them to keep the toxins from entering the hive proper. Best is an air-breathable tarpaulin — moistened if left on for any length of time. Plastic sheets will suffice for a matter of hours only. Be sure to raise the skirts of a plastic covering enough to permit air to circulate once the application is down, but before it is safe to release the bees. Remove the covers as soon as the danger is past.

Symptoms

Poisoned bees will appear paralyzed or may fly or walk erratically. Symptoms may be confused with disease, viral paralysis in particular. But, unlike most diseases of adult bees, a wholesale insecticide poisoning will show up in one or both of two ways:

1. A sudden reduction in forager activity at a hive entrance suggests that bees have been killed in the field by fast-acting toxins. The home population won't be in danger, and the casualties will be quickly replaced by newly maturing house bees, but if mortality is high, honey production will be affected.

2. A large number of dead bees at the entrance indicates a slower-acting poison. The erratic bees have been expelled by house bees to die at the entrance. A great heap of dead bees is enough to break a beekeeper's heart and initiates a less than lighthearted search for a newly sprayed field.

In severe cases, state or federal government compensation on the order of $15 or $20 per colony has been offered to beekeepers. Recourse to legal action may be practical if local insecticide application restrictions or state or federal environmental protection laws have been violated or if a large number of colonies is affected. In agricultural areas, an active and vocal beekeepers' association representing a large membership can be a constructive voice in coordinating beekeeper and farming interests, often before damage is done to the bees.

Practically speaking, an individual small-scale beekeeper's most effective remedy for pesticide poisoning is to identify the source and prevent future contamination. Anticipate pesticide applications and protect your bees.

Afterword

Having gone on at considerable length about getting into beekeeping. I should discuss getting out of it, however briefly.

People leave beekeeping for many reasons, and I won't try to prophesy yours. I was forced out once due to an allergic reaction to stings, twice again due to change of work location; bees aren't transportable across the continent by Mayflower or across the ocean by Alitalia. Each time I had to give up bees the thriving colonies went, gratis, to friends who were eager to take up the hobby.

If you quit, you should be able to sell whole colonies. Run a classified ad in the livestock section of the local paper. Fifty or sixty dollars is a fair price for a single ten-frame hive, complete with a going colony. Supers and woodenware accessories should sell for catalog prices at minimum if in perfect shape. After all, you put your time into assembling and painting the gear, and the bees have worked long hours to construct all that brood comb.

If you can't sell or give colonies away, don't abandon them any more than you'd abandon a pet animal. A fellow in our area tried commercial beekeeping a few years back, and scattered several hundred hives around the county. When he went broke, he just left the bees (and the county). With no attention and lacking the annual bee inspection, the hives became diseased over time. We still find his AFB-contaminated "ghost hives" in overgrown ends of old apple orchards. He would not be welcomed back.

At best, an abandoned colony will diminish and die out. Frames and comb will be turned to a grisly mess by wax moths. At worst, it will become a disease repository, luring successive swarms to perpetuate foulbrood. If you must do away with a thriving colony, be responsible about it. Gas the bees and either bury them, frames and comb and all, or dispose of them in a landfill dump.

But, don't discard your bee veil and smoker, the hive tool, and your harvesting accessories. You'll want them the next time bee fever strikes. And it most surely will.

Appendix A

BEEKEEPING SUPPLIES AND EQUIPMENT

The following is a list of Canadian and American manufacturers and suppliers of beekeeping equipment, plus several overseas firms who sell to the North American market. All offer free catalogs. Most domestic firms also operate retail outlets at their company head-quarters and branches. A visit to the retailer nearest you is a trip well taken; many offer seasonal discounts, special equipment packages at very special prices, even started colonies, complete and ready to go to work for you. All can supply help, information, and personal contacts that are invaluable to the beginning beekeeper.

ARTB Inc.,
C.P. Parc Industrial,
Route Kennedy St. Joseph, Beauce,
Quebec, G0S 2V0,
CANADA

Automated manufacturer of hive bodies, frames, and woodenware including a modern version of Dr. C.C. Miller's (improved) center-entrance full-body feeder, a bee escape that works in any weather, and more. Goods sold KD or assembled and painted. A sheltered workshop under government sponsorship. For Canadians, a free telephone: 800-463-8921.

American Bee Supply, Inc.,
P.O. Box 555, Rt. 7 Sparta Pike,
Lebanon, TN 37088-0555

A new and growing supplier with an unpretentious, hand-drawn catalog and some of the lowest prices around. A beginner's outfit for a little over $50. Worth a drive if you are near Nashville.

B & B Honey Farm,
Rt. 2, Box 245,
Houston, MN 55943

Sells all lines: Root, Dadant, Kelley, and others. Retail store and catalog. Stocked nucs and nine-frame hives with Starline or Italian queens available for pickup toward end of April.

Better Bee,
Route 29,
Greenwich, NY 12834

Full-line mail-order supplier of discount bee gear for the Northeast. Sells ARTB (Quebec) gear. Complete beeswax candle-making supplies. Many unique products including a frame-imbedding wheel that works and a well-selected book list. Honors charge cards.

Bee-Jay Farm,
1524 Drowning Creek Road,
Dacula, GA 30211

Makes hives from rot-resistant red cypress; dovetailed and predrilled and lovely stuff at a justified premium price. Catalog with full line of accessories.

Brushy Mountain Bee Farm, Inc.,
Rt. 1, Box 135,
Moravian Falls, NC 28654

Call 1-800-BEESWAX, free, to order from one of the most innovative catalogs around. Proprietary boxes with a new dual-tenon rabbet joint, undercut hand holds. Brand name goods at discount. Sells ARTB, Inc.'s woodenware.

Cook's Bee Supplies, Ltd.,
91 Edward St.,
Aurora, Ontario L4G 1W1
CANADA

A full-line supplier with branches in Saskatchewan and Prince Edward Island.

Dadant & Sons, Inc.,
Hamilton, IL 62341

The world's largest manufacturer and distributor of bee supplies. Unsurpassed quality. Branches from coast to coast. Sells own brand of Starline Italian hybrid and Midnite Caucasian hybrid bees.

Forbes & Johnson,
P.O. Box 535,
Homerville, GA 31634

From Homerville, "A Honey Of A Place To Live." Sells a full line of utilitarian equipment at about 80 percent of the price of the bigger manufacturers. Hive joints are rabbeted rather than finger-joined (equally strong if glued), in pine or cypress.

Glorybee Bee Box, Inc.,
1015 Arrowsmith St.,
Eugene, OR 97402

Woodenware at discount prices including an exclusive, half-frame "Western Comb Honey," 6⅝" super, complete KD for less than $20. Full line of equipment, by mail. Bees, nucs, and started colonies for pick-up sale in Eugene from early April to mid-May.

Hubbard Apiaries,
P.O. Box 160,
Onsted, MI 49265

and

U.S. 441 South,
Belleview, FL 32620

Makes its own locked-corner hives (complete, less foundation, for under $30), also frames and foundation, extractors, and even its own pollen substitute. Retail or by mail.

F.W. Jones & Son, Ltd.,
44 Dutch St.,
Bedford,
Quebec L0L 1A0
CANADA

The major Canadian supplier since 1878, this company trucks package bees north to Canada each spring. It has twenty-four distribution centers, from Woodville, Nova Scotia, to Lumby, British Columbia. Catalog free upon request.

The Walter T. Kelley Co.,
Clarkson, KY 42726

As advertised, a true "Bee Supply Catalog Supermarket" run by a fellow who's sold what he feels like since 1924, and who isn't bashful about sharing his opinions with his customers. Reasonable prices. There's a cantankerous but refreshing candor in item descriptions.

Robert Lee (bee supplies) Limited,
Beehive Works,
High Street, Cowley,
Uxbridge, Middlesex UB8 2BB
ENGLAND

Hives and V-wired foundation to British standard (a dozen 14"×12" brood frames per super) as well as Langstroth and other hive dimensions. Thomas metalware and such civilized niceties as smoker fuel cartridges. Prices comparable to North American. Catalog free, payment in sterling draft.

Maxant Industries,
28 Harvard Road,
P.O. Box 454,
Ayer, MA 01431

Metal gear primarily for commercial operators: extractors, strainers, and honey tanks. Stainless steel hive tools and smokers that make great gifts.

The A.I. Root Company,
623 West Liberty St.,
P.O. Box 706,
Medina, OH 44258

The second largest U.S. manufacturer of bee supplies of all kinds—none better. Has branch sales offices and independent dealers across the continent. Publishes Gleanings in Bee Culture.

Southwest Bee Supply, Inc.,
3629 North Caballero Place,
Tucson, AZ 85705

A by-mail and retail supplier for the area. Sells California-type migratory equipment, nucs with four drawn frames with brood and food for under $35. Closed Monday and Sunday.

Strauser Bee Supply,
Box 991,
Walla Walla, WA 99362

Full-line western U.S. manufacturer with branches in California and Texas. Stresses accuracy in milling of lower-cost woodenware.

E.H. Thorne (Beehives) Ltd.,
Beehive Works,
Wragby–Lincoln–LN35LA
ENGLAND

Everything for the beekeeper from U.K.-standard "W.B.C." pagoda hives to straw skeps. I couldn't find one of the German-made bee-marking kits (with tiny numbered discs) in this country, and ordered one from Thorne's ads in the U.S. bee journals. The reasonable prices quoted include postage and customs fees.

Ets. Thomas Fils. S.A. B.P. No. 2,
86, Rue Abbe George Thomas,
45450 Fay-Aux-Loges,
FRANCE

A full line of French beekeeping equipment. Catalog in French, prices and payment terms in English translation, but complicated in either language.

H. Van de Kerkhof & Son, Inc.,
4576 Cliffmont Rd.,
North Vancouver,
British Columbia V7G 1J9
CANADA

    Makes a patented twin-walled British-style insulated and ventilated hive in single- and two-queen models.

Western Bee Supplies, Inc.,
P.O. Box 171,
Polson, MT 59860

    Ponderosa pine woodenware (rot-proof cedar for hive covers and bottom boards) at rock-bottom prices. Lowest-priced items sold in large lots only.

Appendix B

BEEKEEPING PERIODICALS

People keep bees on every continent but Antarctica, and in every nation state on earth. The following is a listing of English-language beekeeping journals from around the world. Sample copies of most are free. The two major American magazines are associated with the leading equipment makers. Each features an ad from the competition on its inside front page. That's a nice touch that you don't find in most areas of free enterprise. Dadant & Sons, Inc. is largest in the industry, and its *American Bee Journal* is fairly technical and written for commercial beekeepers, folks with hundreds or thousands of colonies producing honey by the ton. The A.I. Root Company is number two, and does seem to "try harder." A sample copy of its *Gleanings In Bee Culture* should be delivered to you the week you request it. I find *Gleanings* . . . to be well suited to the hobby beekeeper, and the columns by often feuding beekeeping personalities—Richard Taylor's literate but practical views in particular—are worth the subscription cost. Living in New England, I also appreciate the cold-country orientation of *Canadian Beekeeping*. Many regional beekeeper organizations publish area-specific newsletters that can prove invaluable.

American Bee Journal,
Hamilton, IL 62341

Monthly glossy magazine from Dadant & Sons, Inc. for U.S. $10.50 per year, Aus. $16.50. Authoritative. Send for a free copy.

The Australasian Beekeeper,
P.M.B. 19,
Maitland 2320,
NSW,
AUSTRALIA

Monthly, by the beekeepers' association in New South Wales, Queensland, and South Australia. U.S. $15, Aus. and NZ $11.40 a year. Free sample.

The Australian Bee Journal,
Victorian Apiarists' Association,
P.O. Box 426,
Benalia,
Victoria 3672,
AUSTRALIA
  Monthly publication of Victoria beekeepers. Australia $15 local and overseas postpaid per year. Samples free.

An Beachaire (The Irish Beekeeper),
c/o James J. Doran,
St. Jude's Mooncoin,
Waterford,
IRELAND
  Monthly, for U.S. $9, surface postage included.

The Apiarist,
Box 5056,
Papunui,
Christchurch,
NEW ZEALAND
  New Zealand's leading bee journal. Bimonthly for NZ $5 per year.

Bee Craft,
British Beekeepers' Association,
15 West Way,
Copthorne Bank, Crawley,
Sussex, RH10 3DS
ENGLAND
  Official monthly of the BBA. ££5, 10 pence per year postpaid.

Bee World,
International Bee Research Association,
Hill House, Gerrards Cross,
Bucks, SL9 0NR,
ENGLAND
  Quarterly journal of the leading private bee research organization, publisher of expensive but authoritative books on apiculture worldwide. Inquire for prices.

Beekeeping, A West County Journal,
20 Parkhurst Rd.,
Torquay, Devon,
ENGLAND

By and for West County beekeepers. Ten issues a year for U.S. $4 overseas, £1.50 inland.

British Bee Journal,
c/o A.I. Root or direct,
British Bee Publications, Ltd.,
4 Queen St.,
Geddington, Kettering,
Northants NH 14 1AZ,
ENGLAND

A monthly review for ££7 or U.S. $11.25.

Canadian Beekeeping,
Box 128,
Orono, Ontario,
L0B 1M0,
CANADA

"The News Media of the Canadian Honey Industry" at CAN $10 per year. It has a nice home-brewed flavor, includes beekeeping news from Alaska to Cape Breton.

Gleanings In Bee Culture,
623 West Liberty St.,
P.O. Box 706,
Medina, OH 44258-0706

Since 1873 from the A.I. Root Company. Monthly for U.S. $10.35 per year, overseas postage U.S. $3.25 extra. Sample copy free.

Hearthstone Beekeepers Quarterly,
Box 58,
Colinton, Alberta
T0G 0R0,
CANADA

Quarterly for CAN $6.50, U.S. $7 in the USA and abroad.

The Scottish Bee Journal,
34 Rennie St.,
Kilmaronock,
KAl 3AR,
SCOTLAND
Monthly full of practical articles for U.S. $4 per year, postpaid.

Honey Market News,
Market News Branch, F & V Div.,
AMS, USDA, Room 2503-South Bldg.,
14th and Independence Ave., SW,
Washington, DC 20250
Pay $12 for an informative monthly market-intelligence newsletter listing American and imported honey prices, current regional and state-by-state weather reports and their effect on colonies and honey flow, coverage of topical diseases and pest spread and control measures, and by-state CCC Honey Loan Activity in the USA.

Indian Bee Journal,
1325 Sadashiv peth,
Poona 411 030,
INDIA
Quarterly organ of the All India Beekeepers' Association for U.S. $7 by International Mail Order or bank draft payable in Poona. All about working with A. cerana, Indica, and other Indo-Malayan bees.

The New Zealand Beekeeper,
P.O. Box 4048,
Wellington,
NEW ZEALAND
Quarterly at NZ $12.50 per year overseas delivery by seamail.

The Scottish Beekeeper,
19 Drumblair Crescent,
Inverness,
SCOTLAND
Journal of the Scottish Beekeepers' Association. Sample for 20 new pence or equivalent.

The South African Bee Journal,
P.O. Box 47198,
Parklands 2121,
SOUTH AFRICA

Bimonthly of the South African Beekeepers' Association, concentrating on African species. R 12, per year (payable only in twelve S.A. Rands in South Africa).

The Speedy Bee,
P.O. Box 998,
Jesup, GA 31545

Monthly tabloid-size newspaper accenting industry happenings and how-to. A more newsy style than the magazines. U.S. $8 per year in USA, Mexico, and Canada. Add $2 for airmail. U.S. $15 by surface mail overseas. Single copy free.

Country-living interest magazines also run articles on beekeeping. Among the major North American offerings are:

Mother Earth News,
P.O. Box 70,
Hendersonville, NC 28791

TMEN back issues #2, #67, #74, and #92 have excellent bee articles, and others appear regularly.

Harrowsmith,
Camden East,
Ontario, K0K 1J0,
CANADA

Number 60, April/May 1985 includes "Confessions of a Beekeeper." Others on bee subjects from time to time.

B & K's Country Journal,
P.O. Box 392,
Mt. Morris, IL 61054-9956

Occasional bee articles from the leading American country-living magazine.

Organic Gardening,
Emmaus, PA 18099-0003

This food-gardening journal covers pollinators now and again.

Appendix C

BOOK LIST AND INFORMATION SOURCES

More has been written about bees than any other of God's creatures but ourselves, and new material is added to the literature every day.

Here is a list of bee books available from the equipment makers and from selected mail order and retail merchants, unless otherwise indicated. I've commented on the books that I like best, and have added a few lesser-known titles that have proven especially useful or entertaining over the years.

Aebi, Harry, and Aebi, Ormond. **The Art and Adventure of Bee-keeping.** Santa Cruz: Unity Press, 1975. Reprinted by Rodale Press, Emmaus, PA.

The gentle reminiscences of a California "beekeeping bachelor" and his father cited in the Guinness Book of World Records for 404 pounds of honey from a single hive in 1974. That was the year before the book was published with guidance of my old friend and editor, Walter Hard of Garden Way Publishing in Charlotte, Vermont. Not a beginner's how-to manual, but anecdotes arranged in practical subject areas, each story brimming with old-time wisdom and practical insights. Uniquely good on hiving swarms, removing bees from buildings, translating bee's language, and gentling bees. Invaluable for West Coast beekeepers. Direct from the publisher or a bookstore.

Brother Adam. **Bee-Keeping at Buckfast Abbey.** Northants, England: British Bee Publications Ltd., 1975.

Written by the world's preeminent beekeeper, the monk who has kept bees at Buckfast Abbey since acarine disease decimated the British native bees in 1915. Buckfast Italians were used to restock the island nation's apiaries. The book relates the abbey's master system of seasonal management and queen raising. Well worth study by knowledgeable beepeople, but it helps to have a Thorne's or Lee's (England) catalog to be familiar with British Standard twelve-frame equipment. Also tells the experienced winemaker how to make several kinds of mead, a honey wine with origins lost in history. Copies of that rare item, a well-made hardcover, stitched-spine book, signed by the author available from Betterbee and others.

Butler, Colin G. **The World of the Honeybee.** New York: Taplinger, 1975.

Possibly the best book written on bees and their behavior.

Carle, Eric. **The Honeybee and the Robber** New York: Philomel Books, 1981.

Eric lives across the Chickley River Valley from our place, and our bees occasionally trek over to graze on his aspidistra, and vice versa. His beebook is a wonderful pull-tab, moving picture book for lap-sized kids, who will ad lib the sound effects with little prompting. Hummmmm, Bzzzzz, giggle and squirm. In stock at any good bookstore or by mail from the equipment manufacturers.

Coggeshall, William L., and Morse, Roger A. **Beeswax; Production, Harvesting, Processing, and Products.** Ithaca, NY: Wicwas Press, 1984.

This book offers more than anyone but the two apicultural scientists and beekeepers who wrote it could imagine was known about beeswax. Chemistry and mechanics of how bees produce wax; how they and we use it. Such fascinating details as the statements that 100,000 bees working all night can turn out the 800,000 wax scales needed to make a pound of wax; and you'll get about a pound of cappings per 100 pounds of honey produced. This book is $14.95 hard cover or $9.95 paperback, postpaid from Wicwas Press, 25 Hanshaw Rd., Ithaca, NY 14850.

Dadant and Sons, ed. **The Hive and the Honey Bee.** Hamilton, IL: Dadant and Sons, 1976.

The Dadant's 700-plus-page bible of beekeeping. A compendium from twenty-seven experts on all topics. A college text, and exhaustive. Spanish edition available.

Donovan, Robert E. **Hunting Wild Bees.** Tulsa: Winchester Press, 1980.

Hunting bee trees and harvesting wild honey are described as an outdoor sport. Beekeeping fundamentals for non-beekeepers; making and using beehives is described. Photos show cutting a bee tree, harvesting wild honey, and dividing a hollow bee log into gums. The entire stock of this hardcover book was purchased by Root in 1985. It's available at half price: $5.95 plus $.94 postage and handling. Send a check to Root's Windmill Press, Box 1151, Medina, OH 44258, or phone 216-725-6677 for credit card purchases.

Hansen, Henrik. **Honeybee Brood Diseases.** Ithaca, NY: Wicwas Press.

The twenty-five photos in this thirty-two-page book were taken by Danish expert Hansen, and the book was edited by Roger Morse of Cornell. My almost-teen-aged daughter Martha called it "really gross." But it's an effective way to view the enemy in living color.

Heinrich, Bernd. **Bumblebee Economics.** Cambridge, MA: Harvard University Press, 1979.

A marvelous book about a bee species that forages in my home state of Maine cranberry bogs in subfreezing weather, even flying in snowstorms, proving that bees are warmblooded insects of a sort, and better practical economists than most of their human counterparts. Heinrich describes how to attract a queen and raise your own bumblebee nest like kids did in the old days. On order from your bookstore or Harvard University Press.

Jarvis, Dr. D.C. **Folk Medicine.** New York: Fawcett World Library, 1958.

A little paperback from a book written by a practical researcher into Vermont folk medicine. It's full of advice that some brand as quackery or old wives' tales, some think makes a lot of common sense. Values imputed to honey are included among the old-time remedies. If past history is any indicator, much of this will find its way into established medicine in time. Buy it from equipment sellers.

Jaycox, Elbert R. **Beekeeping in the Midwest.** Urbana, IL: University of Illinois at Urbana-Champaign College of Agriculture.

This has an unfortunate title, but offers comprehensive and knowledgeable advice applicable throughout North America and the temperate climate zones of the world. It's written by a leading bee scientist with a practical, no-nonsense perspective. His recommendations for his home-state specialty of the time, the Dadant size, 6⅝" Illinois extracting super, seem less than enthusiastic, and for that reason alone I trust what he writes. It's available at little or no charge from many Extension offices, or for about $8 from Dadant and others.

Kelley, Walter T. **How to Keep Bees and Sell Honey.** Clarkson, KY: Walter Kelley Co., 1985.

This is the same Mr. Kelley who makes bee equipment and who will refund a nickel if you overpay (and charge you right quick if you underpay). The book is delightfully 1940ish in tone and full of Mr. Kelley's opinions. You may not agree with all of them, but you'll benefit from the reading. The most enjoyable of the beginners' books. It tells how bees can finance your winters in Florida. Buy it from Kelley's company.

Laidlaw, Harry H. **Contemporary Queen Rearing.** Hamilton, IL: Dadant and Sons, 1979.

One of the Dadant library and a standard text on raising and shipping both queens and package bees, this book is well illustrated and photographed and has a super reference list. Buy it from Dadant and others. You'll also want Dr. Laidlaw's **Instrumental Insemination of Honeybee Queens** so you can pick your drones. Queen rearing is a real specialty, and it's a good idea to read up before trying it yourself. With Ottawa forever debating quarantines on foreign queens and package bees, Canadian beekeepers in particular might be smart to read these two books. They're hard reading, but authoritative and the best there is on the subject.

Laidlaw, Harry H., and Eckert, J.E. **Queen Rearing.** Berkeley, CA: University of California, 1962.

This book covers the topic in under 200 pages. It may be available through your library. If not, order it from a bookstore or the publisher.

Lindauer, Martin H. **Communication Among Social Bees.** Cambridge, MA: Harvard University Press, 1961.

The first edition of this 161-page book got me turned on to bees back in my college days. A disciple of Karl von Frisch, who first recognized the language of bees, Lindauer describes the bee's nectar-location dance in fine prose and with an infectious excitement that's lacking in most scientific works. Buy it from your bookseller or the publisher.

Longgood, William. **The Queen Must Die.** New York: Norton, 1958.

This book is written by a Cape Cod beekeeper whose anthropomorphic characterizations of **A. mellifera** may grate on your literary sensibilities, but who does love his bees. It's especially good for your non-beekeeping friends who wonder why you risk those stings.

Matheson, Andrew. **Practical Beekeeping in New Zealand.** Wellington: Government Printer.

Here's an outstanding beekeeping manual combining science and practical how-to. It's packed with unique insights and tips. Examples: turn your lawn sprinkler on hives being robbed. Simulated rain will send robbers home. Drone brood in worker cells and excessive drones in the fall indicate a failing queen needing replacement. This new and attractive paperback is by a graduate entomologist. The material is largely applicable to North America, but remember that New Zealand is in the southern hemisphere, so it's spring there when it is fall here. The price is NZ $32, or $15 in U.S. money at 1985 exchange rates. A personal check will be accepted, and service is reasonable fast by seamail. From Government Printing Office, Private Bag, Wellington, New Zealand.

McDowell, Robert. **The Africanized Honeybee in the United States: What Will Happen to the U.S. Beekeeping Industry?** Agricultural Economic Report 519. Washington: U.S. Department of Agriculture.

A November, 1984 research report analyzing potential economic impact on the beekeeping industry of the inevitable invasion of North America by the Brazilian/ African killer bees. The book offers four scenarios, none of them especially encouraging, predicting losses to beekeeping ranging from $26 million to $58 million. The loss of 90 percent of the package bee and queen raising output is predicted in all four scenarios. Buy this from the Superintendent of Documents, Washington, DC 20402, Betterbee, and others.

McGregor, S.E. **Insect Pollination of Cultivated Crop Plants.** Washington: U.S. Government Printing Office.

This is an authoritative and exhaustive treatment of the topic that will tell you what bee forage to expect from local farms. Cost is $12 postpaid. Order number 001-000-03549-5.

Michener, Charles D. **The Social Behavior of the Bees.** Cambridge, MA: Belknap Press of Harvard University Press, 1974.

Another 450-plus-page book, a $40 monument, but it's well worth checking out from the library for winter reading.

Miller, Dr. C.C. **Fifty Years Among the Bees.** New Berlin, NY: 1915 edition reprinted by the Molly Yes Press, 1980.

The book has a preface by E.R. Root, who visited the erudite Dr. Miller in 1920, a few months before the author died in his ninety-ninth year. This book offers proof if we need it that there's precious little new under the sun. Dr. Miller, who never practiced medicine due to poor health, but who took up hauling seventy-pound beehives instead, rambles on entertainingly about a beekeeper's life in upper New York State in the 1880s and on for a half-century. The book is packed with old-time tips and ideas from the era when the Langstroth hive design was being fine-tuned and every beekeeper was an Edison-era inventor. You'll find a practical skeptic's view of nineteenth century versions of gadgets (slatted bottom boards and double-queen hives) and gimmicks (Demaree no-swarm plan and shaken swarms for comb honey) being touted today as newfound wisdom. A gentle book for entertaining bedtime reading, but keep a notebook handy.

Morse, Roger A. **Rearing Queen Honeybees.** Ithaca, NY: Wicwas Press, 1979.

This book by the professor of apiculture at Cornell covers the subject in 128 pages. Morse is also author of **The Complete Guide to Beekeeping,** *published in 1972 by E. P. Dutton and Co., New York, and revised in 1980.*

Natural Therapeutics Series with titles on honey, pollen, royal jelly, and propolis. Paris: La Librarie Maloine, 1983.

Scientific and medical foundations (such as they are) of bee products as human health-enhancers. Do you suffer from a neuro-vegetative imbalance? How about anemia, anorexia, arteriosclerosis, flu, frigidity, hepato-vascular difficulties, impotence, neurasthenia, senescence, ulcers, or Down's syndrome? These are just some problems that the author, Dr. Yves Donadieu, claims can be influenced by royal jelly, and that's just one book in the series.

It makes me glad for United States and Canadian governmental food and drug regulations. Books are available by mail from the publisher at 27 Rue de l'Ecole-de-Medecine, 75006, in Paris.

Root, A.I. et al. **ABC and XYZ of Bee Culture.** Medina, OH: A. I. Root Co., 1978.

*A 700-plus-page encyclopedia based on Mr. Root's original 1877 volume, updated periodically with original material from **Gleanings In Bee Culture**, this book is approaching its fortieth edition. It's a little uneven, with some segments out of date, but it's crammed with information, opinions, and fact and fancy of beekeeping. It is also available in the 1890 edition of 400-plus pages.*

Seeley, Thomas D., and Morse, Roger A. **Bait Hives for Honeybees.** Ithaca, NY: Cornell University.

This book is the result of several years of research by two top academic bee experts. It tells how and why honeybees swarm, how to lure them into boxes placed in the open, then transfer them to conventional hives. This six-page pamphlet is available for $1.25 from Distribution Center C, 7 Research Park, Cornell University, Ithaca, NY 14850.

Snodgrass, Robert E. **Anatomy of the Honeybee.** Ithaca, NY: Comstock Publishing Co., Cornell University, 1956.

Bees haven't changed since this comprehensive text was published. Your library or the state library system should have a copy. It's interesting to see just where those tracheal mites hide out, in case you want to do some microscope work of your own.

Taylor, Richard. **The Joys of Beekeeping.** New York: St. Martin's Press, 1974.

You'll enjoy these observations plus how-to offered by Dr. Taylor, columnist for **Gleanings In Bee Culture**, *and a philosopher-beekeeper who combines a hard-nosed practicality with a thoughtful reverence for simple living in harmony with nature. Henry Thoreau would approve of this book.*

Taylor, Richard. **The New Comb Honey Book.** Interlaken, NY: Linden Books, 1981.

This book is a guide to beekeeping, stressing techniques of producing comb honey. A man of strong opinions, Dr. Taylor, but whether you agree with him or not, his views are based on years of successful beekeeping. Order it direct or from bee suppliers.

United States Government Printing Office. **Beekeeping in the United States,** USDA Handbook 335. Washington, DC: Government Printing Office.

Here's a compendium of tightly written articles on a broad range of topics by the USDA apiculture specialists from several bee experiment stations. It doesn't tell you how to do things; rather, it implies why you should. Limited quantities are available for a dollar or two from some Extension Service offices. The book is not out of print as has been reported; the government just wants you to pay for it now. Send a check for $7.50 or your credit card number and a signature approving a $7.50 charge to Superintendent of Documents, U.S. Government Printing Office, Washington, DC 20402 and ask for one copy of Publication 1981-0-349-986, stock number 001-000-04137-1. Be prepared to wait a bit, but no as long as you used to.

Von Frisch, Karl. **The Dance Language and Orientation of Bees.** Translated by Leigh E. Chadwick, Jr., Cambridge, MA: Belknap Press of Harvard University Press, 1967.

Here's a book that is utterly impractical and hard reading, but absorbing and a landmark book in literature. Get it from your library, some suppliers, or the publisher, for about $40.

Von Frisch, Karl. **The Dancing Bees.** Cambridge, MA: Harvard University Press, 1961.

A passable translation from von Frisch's German original 1953 synopsis of his world-beating bee communications research. This good, if small-print and academic volume on all aspects of bee behavior is by the master himself.

Wilhelm, Maxine. **Wick, Wax and Talk, 2nd Time Around.** Clarkson, KY: Walter T. Kelley, Co.

This twenty-eight-page pamphlet includes everything a beginning candle maker needs to know.

Wilson, Edward O. **The Insect Societies.** Cambridge, MA: Belknap Press of Harvard University Press, 1971.

*This book tells all about how bees, ants, and their relatives carry on their complex, interdependent lives. The fifty-four-page bibliography alone is worth the price. If you like this really big Harvard Paperback book, you'll also like Professor Wilson's book, **On Human Nature**, also from Harvard.*

INDEX

Numbers in italics refer to illustrations.

More Good Books from

✸ WILLIAMSON PUBLISHING

PRACTICAL POLE BUILDING CONSTRUCTION
by Leigh Seddon
   Saves money, time, labor; no excavation. Complete how-to-build information with *original* architectural plans and specs for small barn, horse barn, shed, animal shelter, cabins and more.

176 pages, 8½×11, over 100 architectural renderings, tables, charts. Quality paperback, $10.95

THE SHEEP RAISER'S MANUAL
by William Kruesi
   "Don't raise sheep without it."
                    The New Farm

   "Overall, *The Sheep Raiser's Manual* does a better job of integrating all aspects of sheep farming into a successful sheep enterprise than any other book published in the United States."
                    Dr. Paul Saenger
                    New England Farmer

                    280 pages, 6×9, illustrations, photos, charts & tables. Quality paperback, $13.95.

RAISING POULTRY SUCCESSFULLY
by Will Graves
   "An easy-to-understand beginner's guide to raising chickens, ducks, and geese. A good choice . . ."
                    Library Journal

   Complete how-to for raising meat only, eggs only or a dual purpose flock. Warmly and expertly written.

196 pages, 6×9, illustrations, photos, tables.
Quality paperback, $9.95

RAISING PIGS SUCCESSFULLY
by Kathy and Bob Kellogg

Everything you need to know for the perfect low-cost, low-work pig raising operation. Choosing piglets, to housing, feeds, care, breeding, slaughtering, packaging, and even cooking your home grown pork.

224 pages, 6×9, illustrations, photos, tables.
Quality paperback, $9.95

RAISING RABBITS SUCCESSFULLY
by Bob Bennett

"Here is one of the better books on raising rabbits."
Booklist

Written by one of the foremost rabbit authorities, this book is ideal for the beginning rabbit raiser, raising for food, fun, shows and profit.

192 pages, 6×9, illustrations and photos.
Quality paperback, $9.95

SUMMER IN A JAR: MAKING PICKLES, JAMS & MORE
by Andrea Chesman

"With recipes this simple and varied, it's hard to find an excuse not to preserve summer in one's cupboard."
Publishers Weekly

Chesman introduces single jar recipes so you can make pickles and relishes a single quart at a time. Plenty of low-sugar jams, marmalades, relishes. Pickles by the crock, too. Outstanding recipes.

160 pages, 8¼×7¼, illustrations.
Quality paperback, $8.95

GOLDE'S HOMEMADE COOKIES
by Golde Hoffman Soloway

"Cookies are her chosen realm and how sweet a world it is to visit."
Publishers Weekly

Over 100 treasured recipes that defy description. Suffice it to say that no one could walk away from Golde's cookies without asking for another . . . plus the recipe.

144 pages, 8¼×7¼, illustrations.
Quality paperback, $8.95

THE BROWN BAG COOKBOOK: NUTRITIOUS PORTABLE LUNCHES FOR KIDS AND GROWN-UPS
by Sara Sloan

Here are more than 1,000 brown bag lunch ideas with 150 recipes for simple, quick, nutritious lunches.

192 pages, 8¼ × 7¼, illustrations.
Quality paperback, $9.95

HOME TANNING & LEATHERCRAFT SIMPLIFIED
by Kathy Kellogg

"An exceptionally thorough and readable do-it-yourself book."
Library Journal

192 pages, 6×9, step-by-step illustrations, photos, tanning recipes.
Quality paperback, $9.95

BUILDING FENCES
Of Wood, Stone, Metal & Plants
by John Vivian

Fencing in, fencing out or simply enhancing your place—John Vivian shows how to make just about every kind of fence. Wood fence, stone fence, brick & block fence, hedgerow, iron fence, privacy screen, farm fence, wire fence, electric fence and hi-tensile fence. Lots on gates, working with cement and mortar, tools. As solid a how-to book as one could ever hope for and a pure delight to read and use.

188 pages, 8½ × 11, photos, step-by-step illustrations
Quality paperback, $13.95

TO ORDER

At your bookstore or order directly from Williamson Publishing. We accept Visa or Mastercard (please include number, expiration date and signature), or send check to **Williamson Publishing Co., Church Hill Road, P.O. Box 185, Charlotte, Vermont 05445.** (Phone orders: 800-234-8791). Please add $3.20 for postage and handling. Satisfaction guaranteed or full refund without questions or quibbles.

WILLIAMSON PUBLISHING CO.

BOX 185, CHURCH HILL ROAD,
CHARLOTTE, VERMONT 05445